THE
Memphis, Clarksville & Louisville
RAILROAD

THE
Memphis, Clarksville & Louisville
RAILROAD

• A HISTORY •

Todd DeFeo

THE
History
PRESS

Published by The History Press
Charleston, SC
www.historypress.net

Front cover: (*top*) Nashville, Tennessee, pictured here in 1864, was an important logistics hub during the Civil War. The Tennessee state capitol is visible in the background. *Library of Congress*; (*bottom*) A bird's-eye view of the city of Clarksville as depicted in 1870. The railroad bridge across the Cumberland River is at lower right. *Library of Congress*.

Back cover: (*top*) Fighting during the Civil War wreaked havoc on railroads. Here, workers near Murfreesboro, Tennessee, repair a section of track after the Battle of Stones River in 1863—this was a common scene across the South in the wake of fighting. *Library of Congress*; (*bottom*) The historic L&N depot, pictured here in 2012, stands in downtown Clarksville at the intersection of Commerce and Tenth Streets. *Railfanning.org*.

First published 2019

Manufactured in the United States

ISBN 9781467143462

Library of Congress Control Number: 2019945056

Notice: The information in this book is true and complete to the best of our knowledge. It is offered without guarantee on the part of the author or The History Press. The author and The History Press disclaim all liability in connection with the use of this book.

This book is dedicated to my lovely wife, Ruth. Thank you for traipsing across the world with me and for letting me visit so many train museums.

And to our son, Thomas. You'll be with me "Everywhere I Go."

Contents

ACKNOWLEDGEMENTS

T his book builds on work started around 2002. Such a work is merely a draft and will never be completed. A huge thank you goes to "Hey You" and K4DS for reviewing and editing this work.

INTRODUCTION

The Memphis, Clarksville & Louisville Railroad's "good old days" were rather short-lived.

Many histories mention—usually briefly—the Memphis, Clarksville & Louisville (MC&L) Railroad, but few records of the railroad seem to exist, and the accounts that do are incomplete. So, writing a history of this railroad required weaving together a narrative based on limited files and news accounts.

Perhaps that is what makes this road such an intriguing study. There is no complete history solely dedicated to this line. The line was inextricably linked to the much larger Louisville & Nashville (L&N) Railroad from the start. The accounts of the MC&L that exist explore the railroad in the context of the L&N.

It is essential to first recognize its geography. The railroad was the middle section of a line between Louisville and Nashville. The MC&L built a link between Paris, Tennessee, and the Tennessee-Kentucky state line; the community that grew up in the area was known as State Line during the early railroad era. A community in this area, Guthrie, Kentucky, first developed along a stagecoach line in the 1840s. Guthrie, named for L&N president James Guthrie, formally incorporated in 1876.

I first learned of the road in 2002, and it was intriguing to me from the start. I wrote an article for the local newspaper in 2003 in honor of the 135th anniversary of the February 1868 strike that spelled doom for the line, which had struggled to operate from its inception.

As a company, the railroad existed for roughly two decades—from 1852 until 1871. The company only operated the entire eighty-two-mile-long line under the cloud of war or under receivership starting at the time of its completion in 1861. After the Civil War, it ran in receivership, and the larger L&N, which overshadowed it for its entire corporate history—and supported the MC&L—subsumed the "Clarksville" in the decade after the Civil War.

Creating this account proved to be somewhat challenging given the dearth of reliable and available information. It was written using newspaper accounts and corroborated with official railroad records and government reports where possible. I have made attempts to correct the spellings of names, but at times, this information was inconsistent or otherwise unavailable.

Even the line's completion date is open to some conjecture. Most accounts say it was completed in mid-April 1861, just as the Civil War commenced. But news accounts from November 1861 indicate that is when the first train rolled over the Tennessee River bridge, after the last link of the railroad was completed.

Sometimes history leaves us an incomplete record from which to work. That is what happened here. I have presented information as accurately as possible. It is vital to remember roads such as the Memphis, Clarksville & Louisville, even if most histories have opted to relegate this line to nothing more than a brief mention.

Gateway to the New South

By all accounts, August 6, 1860, started as a typical Monday. But by the time Benjamin Bartle eased the locomotive W.B. Munford onto the bridge crossing the Cumberland River in Clarksville, Tennessee, he was entering the annals of history. His train was the first to cross the bridge, a major hurdle in building a vital portion of the rail line linking Memphis and Louisville.

During the day, word spread throughout the town that a train would cross the bridge that evening. Crowds gathered to witness this moment nearly a decade in the making. The excitement was assuredly palpable. The locomotive, a steam engine of typical size for its day, pulled a single passenger coach for the journey. About a dozen participants "mounted upon the engine and tender"[1] to be a part of the historic first ride. Hundreds more wanted to participate; one account indicates they rode in a car behind the locomotive, while another says they succumbed to their fears and watched from terra firma.

The crossing was a success. And while it marked the conquering of a natural obstacle along the Memphis, Clarksville & Louisville Railroad's route, it was equally noteworthy that this development came less than a century after the first permanent settlement in the area. People today see this remarkable bridge spanning the river and recognize it as a landmark of Clarksville, but few realize its history and the role it played in the completion of a vital railroad link between Memphis and Louisville.

Standing on Tenth Street in downtown Clarksville, it may be hard to imagine this was a bustling transportation hub in the mid-nineteenth century. Passenger trains no longer travel through the city, and freight trains seldom pass through, either. But the tracks are there, and they are still in use. The old depot, known to locals as the L&N (Louisville & Nashville) Station, still stands, but it no longer serves weary travelers stepping off a train from Louisville or passengers ready to begin a trip.

Trains that run on these tracks operate over the last remaining vestige of the Memphis, Clarksville & Louisville (MC&L) Railroad. Contemporaries ridiculed the route as "beginning in the woods and ending in a hollow tree."[2] The road was chartered in 1852 and ran from Paris, Tennessee, to the Tennessee-Kentucky state line (known as State Line). Like so many railroads of its day, the MC&L's name suggested its larger route, and of the three cities in the line's name, Clarksville was the only town it directly served.

It was a spoke in the wheel of a more extensive network and one of three that made up the vital rail link between Louisville, Kentucky, and Memphis, Tennessee, that connected the Mississippi and Ohio Rivers. At Paris, Tennessee, it connected with the Memphis & Ohio Railroad, which completed the run to Memphis. At State Line, the MC&L interchanged with the L&N, which operated to Bowling Green, Kentucky, via Russellville, Kentucky. There, it merged with the L&N main line between Louisville, Kentucky, and Nashville, Tennessee.

"Thus three independent railway projects were constructed, but in reality a single system had come into existence," Thomas Dionysius Clark, a Mississippi native perhaps best remembered for his 1937 work, *A History of Kentucky*, wrote in his 1933 history of the L&N.[3] "It was impossible to develop the resources of the country from which the wealth of any road leading out of Louisville would have to come without building in the direction of Memphis and Nashville. The completion of direct connections between these two southern commercial centers was the realization of a dream of the fondest promoters who pushed their projects through to the finish despite hardships, financial reverses, and many times a total lack of local support and appreciation."

Clark added: "When the three roads were placed in operation, it was immediately seen that it was imperative they should be operated as one trunk system."

In many ways, the trio was greater than the sum of its parts. The MC&L existed for about twenty years—from 1852 until 1871—and only operated its entire eighty-two-mile line for about three years (about a year starting in 1861 and again from August 1866 until February 1868). After that, the L&N leased the line before purchasing it in 1871.

In studying the MC&L, it is necessary to recognize the road would not have existed if not for its connections with other lines. Following a strike in February 1868, the MC&L fell under the control of the larger and more influential L&N. By the latter half of the 1860s, the MC&L's and the L&N's collective histories became entwined.

Perhaps it was historian Maury Klein who best summed up the road when he said the MC&L "seemed like one more piece in a bewildering jigsaw puzzle."[4]

Still, the MC&L is very much a microcosm of the railroad story of the mid-nineteenth century. To be sure, it shortened the time it took to travel between the major economic cities of Louisville and Memphis. But the railroad's ability to make money didn't match its founders' aspirations.

The MC&L predates the Civil War, and the war demonstrated its strategic importance to the region. During the conflict, its tracks fell into disarray, and the company revitalized the route only to run out of money. A century later, railroads again fell into disfavor; passenger service declined, and automobiles became the favored mode of transportation for millions of Americans.

Time and time again, the tracks were rebuilt, providing for a central theme that repeats itself throughout the 160-plus-year history of the MC&L and its successors. If rising from the literal and proverbial ashes is one central theme, a lack of resources is another. Whatever excitement residents had for the rail link, capital never seemed to match that enthusiasm.

Perhaps Clarksville makes for the perfect case study of how railroads shaped a community. At one point, three lines passed through the city. The first one dates to before the Civil War. Two others bisected the town following the war. Today, the only one that remains is the former MC&L—the first rail company to serve the city. While many retellings of the city's history focus on the role the Cumberland River played in its development, the railroad was similarly instrumental in developing Clarksville into the community it is today.

A Louisville & Nashville successor, CSX Transportation, sold the line in the 1980s to short-line operator R.J. Corman. A portion of the former MC&L between Cumberland City, Tennessee, and Guthrie, Kentucky, is now part of R.J. Corman's 113-mile-long Memphis Line. The road no longer reaches Memphis, but the line's name harkens back to a time when the tracks were a gateway to Memphis and the Mississippi River, which connected other significant ports, such as New Orleans.

The MC&L is often overlooked and, at best, remembered as part of the family tree of the modern CSX Transportation's predecessors and overshadowed by the larger L&N. But its importance to the region is enormous. It is the first line that served Clarksville and other communities, such as Cumberland City and Palmyra, Tennessee—communities that are still somewhat off the beaten trail. The railroad shortened the distance and provided a quicker connection to major destinations in the region and larger cities, including New Orleans and Cincinnati.[5]

The line came to life during a decade of nationwide railroad expansion, when citizens of every community, town and city wanted to jump into the railroad game. It was far from the earliest of railroads established in the country. Travel during the mid-nineteenth century was slow and potentially dangerous. The MC&L encountered troubles and reinvented itself, as so many railroads around the country did at that time. Despite its rough times, the route is a survivor.

Road to the Rail

In 1850, there were more than nine thousand miles of railroad tracks in the United States—more than three times the mileage in the country a decade earlier. A majority of those tracks ran through the northern and mid-Atlantic states. Tennessee had no railroads at the time.

Large portions of the state were still undeveloped less than a century earlier. Understanding how the region developed in its early years is imperative to understanding the community that created the Memphis, Clarksville & Louisville.

Native Americans—including the Archaic, Woodland and Mississippian cultures—settled in what is today Middle Tennessee starting thousands of years ago. The Cumberland River was the lifeline for early civilizations and settlers in the area. The French learned of the river in the 1670s and named it "Riviere des Chauouanons" for the Shawnees, a Native American society that hunted and traded along the waterway.[6] However, it was Dr. Thomas Walker, a Virginia native, who gave the river its permanent name. While traveling with a group of explorers, he renamed the river in 1750 in honor of William Augustus, the Duke of Cumberland.[7]

In the waning years of the eighteenth century, the area that became known as Middle Tennessee was sparsely populated. Among the explorers to pass through the area was John Montgomery, a famed soldier and explorer, who arrived during a hunting expedition in the 1770s. During this same era,

A statue of John Montgomery, an officer during the American Revolution who is credited with founding Clarksville and Montgomery, stands in downtown Clarksville, as shown in this photograph taken on November 9, 2012. *Railfanning.org.*

James Robertson led a group from eastern Tennessee to Big Salt Lick on the Cumberland River, an area that is now part of Nashville.

Moses Renfroe was perhaps the first European to establish a settlement in Montgomery County when he did so around 1780. Valentine Sevier, whose older brother John served as the first and third governor of the state of Tennessee, established another early settlement around 1792; he built a small rock fort where he and his family could take refuge from Native American attacks.

Around this time, John Montgomery, the man for whom Montgomery County is named, identified the area near the confluence of the Cumberland and Red Rivers as the ideal location to create a permanent settlement. The area "had the advantages of two rivers, good landings, and…a gushing spring of pure water, and these were sufficient to tempt the pioneer to it."[8] Montgomery and Martin Armstrong laid out the two-hundred-acre town plan for Clarksville, and the two named the new settlement for George Rogers Clark, a Virginian who was a high-ranking officer on the northwestern frontier during the Revolutionary War.[9]

A building said to be Sevier Station, an early settlement in Clarksville, is shown on November 9, 2012. *Railfanning.org.*

Tennessee gained its statehood in 1796, breaking off from North Carolina.[10] By then, the area was noted for its tobacco crop, and because of this notoriety, in 1788, the North Carolina General Assembly established a tobacco inspection facility in Clarksville. "The fact is only remarkable as showing how early the cultivation of tobacco came to be an important industry around Clarksville, and as marking the inception of a tobacco market, which may be claimed with justice to be second in the United States," W.P. Titus noted in his 1887 history, *Picturesque Clarksville, Past and Present: A History of the City of the Hills.* It would also help drive a desire to improve transportation in the area for the better part of the next century.

The early settlers focused their efforts on building the essential infrastructure needed for a community, including roads, churches and schools.[11] The town's development took another step forward when James Adams built the county's courthouse—a log structure—in the 1790s. Other courthouses followed, including one built after the Great Fire of 1878—the building that currently stands as the centerpiece of downtown Clarksville.

In telling the history of Clarksville, many focus on the river as a catalyst for the city's growth. To be sure, the river helped the region mature economically and transported tobacco produced in the area to destinations far and wide,

Above: Because of the volume of traffic that passed through Clarksville, in 1898, the federal government built a customs house and post office at the corner of Second and Commerce Streets to process the increasing volumes of mail heading into and out of the city. In 1984, the building, pictured here around 1971, was transformed into the Customs House Museum and Cultural Center. *Library of Congress*.

Right: The Montgomery County Courthouse, built in 1878, is shown as it appeared around 2002 during its reconstruction following the devastating 1999 tornado. The courthouse was rebuilt following a fire in 1900 and after the 1999 tornado. *Railfanning.org*.

including Pittsburgh and New Orleans. The region was once among the largest markets for a type of dark-fired tobacco that was famous the world over and known as "Clarksville tobacco." One of the city's newspapers was even named the *Tobacco Leaf*. Tobacco was the impetus for wanting to improve and expand the area's transportation network.[12]

The Railroad Movement

The movement to develop railroads in the Volunteer State dates to January 1830, when the state senate approved a measure to support state aid for internal improvements. On December 8, 1831, the state legislature incorporated the Clarksville & Russellville Railroad. Ultimately, however, the railroad was unable to secure the capital needed and forfeited its charter. While the early 1830s were a period of economic prosperity, railroad projects in the state ultimately slowed in the wake of the Panic of 1837, a financial crisis that lasted until the mid-1840s.[13]

By 1838–39, forty-three steamboats were traveling to Clarksville and Nashville.[14] One prominent reminder of the city's river traffic days remains on the side of the Poston building, constructed by John H. Poston, in downtown Clarksville. In the 1870s, an enterprising party painted an advertisement on the side of the building, which had the same effect as a modern-day billboard situated along the side of the highway.

When railroad fever struck the city by 1843, citizens bandied about the idea of a line connecting Clarksville and Hopkinsville, Kentucky, and eventually other points.[15] But the "project fell completely through for want of means caused by the great lack of public interest."[16]

Talk of railroads forming in cities across the country filled the pages of Tennessee's newspapers. Six years later, interest grew among Clarksville's residents for a line connecting Louisville and Memphis.

In 1840, Memphis had a population of a mere 1,800 residents, while Louisville boasted a population of more than 21,000. By 1846, Clarksville had more than 1,100 residents. Despite their population differences, all three cities had one significant commonality—they were river cities, which provided the original impetus for their development.

While the interest among Clarksville residents was not significant enough to bring a railroad to fruition, in April 1846, residents of Hopkinsville, Kentucky, gathered to discuss creating a connection from their city to the

A view of the Poston Building in downtown Clarksville in November 1971. In the 1870s, an advertisement was painted on the building's side; this is still visible. Much like a billboard situated along the side of the interstate, the ad was visible to passing river traffic. *Library of Congress*.

Cumberland River. "We trust the people of Clarksville and Montgomery county will pay due attention to these movements, and they will not fail to take such measures as will secure an efficient representation of their interests and views," reported the *Clarksville Chronicle*.[17]

The *Clarksville Chronicle* informed its readers that building a railroad would cost $20,000 per mile (nearly $655,000 in 2018 dollars), while a turnpike would cost a mere $4,000 per mile.[18] Regardless, Hopkinsville residents opted to build a line to Eddyville, Kentucky, on the Cumberland River, skipping Clarksville.[19] However, that track was never laid.

Eventually, a railroad was established that connected Henderson, Kentucky, and Nashville, Tennessee. Initial plans called for the road to pass through Clarksville. However, its route changed, and Clarksville was no longer along the road's projected course.

"Had the projectors—some of them the most prominent citizens of Clarksville—listened to the advice of far-seeing men, who look forward for

Gustavus Adolphus Henry (1804–1880) was a Whig Party leader and a law school classmate of future Confederate president Jefferson Davis. Henry, nicknamed the "Eagle Orator of Tennessee," ran for governor of Tennessee in 1853 but lost the election to Democrat Andrew Johnson. During the Civil War, he served for three years in the Confederate Senate. *HathiTrust*.

results…and divided the subscriptions between the two roads, Clarksville would now be a prosperous commercial and manufacturing city with a population at least four times as large as that given by the last census," wrote prominent Clarksville resident John W. Faxon in 1881.[20]

In 1850, the state legislature chartered a line between Clarksville and Madisonville, Kentucky. Despite discussions about the need for railroads in the state, there were no railroads in Tennessee in 1850. In response, Tennessee officials seriously committed to building them. A decade later, the state had 1,200 miles of rail in operation. On March 5, 1850, the Commonwealth of Kentucky chartered the Louisville & Nashville (L&N). The charter provided for a branch line to Memphis. The branch would diverge from the main line five miles south of Bowling Green. Thus, the idea of bringing a railroad to Clarksville was alive—and it seemed likely. A meeting in Clarksville on May 10, 1851, brought together a group of citizens who were in favor of a railroad. The group elected G.A. Henry as president and agreed that a railroad convention was in order.

On May 14, 1851, the *Clarksville Jeffersonian* reported:

> *On the first meeting of the Corresponding Committee in favor of the Clarksville, Memphis and Louisville Rail-road, in Clarksville on the 10th of May, 1851, G. A. Henry, Esq. was appointed the President of said committee, whereupon, it was unanimously*

> *Resolved, That the friends of said Road along the whole line hold a Rail-road Convention in the town of Clarksville, being nearly central, and easy of access by water from the extreme points of the contemplated Rail-road, for the purpose of taking into consideration the importance of initial steps for the building of said Road, and devising the ways and means of accomplishing the same. It was farther*
>
> *Resolved, That said committee, after consulting the friends of the Road as to the best time of holding said Convention, settle on the day when it shall be held, and give timely notice of the same through the newspapers at Memphis, Clarksville, Louisville and all intermediate points.*[21]

With this action, the drive to bring a railroad to Clarksville had picked up steam, and in about a year, the city of Clarksville would formally be in the railroad business.

In the Woods

On January 28, 1852, the Tennessee state legislature granted a charter for the Memphis, Clarksville & Louisville (MC&L) Railroad. Lawmakers gave the new company the "power to unite with any company" the legislature in Kentucky might charter to build a railroad from either Louisville or "some suitable point" on the line between Nashville and Louisville.[22]

The legislature gave railroad officials "ten years to complete said road, and five years to complete that part of said road from Clarksville to the Kentucky line, or to the junction with the Louisville and Nashville rail road on to the city of Louisville."

The railroad began with capital stock of $3 million divided into shares of $100. The legislature authorized the company to increase its capital stock to $4 million. The act named eleven members to a board of commissioners: Robert M. House, Edmund Howard, John S. Hart, Newton Hollingsworth, J. Anderson, Robt. W. McClure, Robt. G. Johnson, Geo. W. Hampton, N.H. Allen, William Dudley and Jas. E. Bailey. The state granted the board the power to act and manage the railroad's affairs "until it shall be organized by the election of a board of directors," which the company could do as soon as $50,000 of stock was subscribed.

Less than a month after the MC&L was formed, on February 4, 1852, the Tennessee state legislature chartered the Nashville & Memphis Railroad, sometimes called the Nashville & Tennessee Railroad, to build a line between Memphis and Paris, Tennessee, roughly 60 miles west of Clarksville and 130 miles east of Memphis. It was later renamed the Memphis & Ohio and would ultimately connect with the MC&L at Paris.[23] The state followed up on February 11, 1852, with an act to establish a system of internal improvements that provided for $8,000 per mile in state bonds. Railroads received the money when they received subscriptions to fund construction, including grading construction of bridges and preparation for the laying of tracks.[24]

A Memphis-to-Louisville line via Clarksville ultimately won favor among movers and shakers in Memphis who feared giving too much power to their counterparts in Nashville. "The Memphis merchants were much given to petty jealousies, and already they had protested building a railroad to Nashville; they feared by doing so they would assist Nashville in her efforts to become the empire city of the state," wrote historian Thomas Dionysius Clark.[25]

"This idea of connecting Louisville and Memphis originated in Memphis as the result of a desire on the part of the merchants of that place to tap the trade which normally went to Nashville at its source," Clark added. "At the same time the Memphis merchants were agitating for a railroad from Memphis to Louisville, the Louisville merchants were equally anxious to build from Louisville to Memphis."

As the MC&L and the Memphis & Ohio worked to build their respective sections, the L&N worked to construct a third segment of the Memphis line starting at Memphis Junction, roughly four miles south of Bowling Green, and working toward State Line.[26]

Action on the MC&L railroad ramped up on April 5 and 6, 1852, when interested citizens met in Clarksville to discuss the railroad. On the first day, the group resolved:

> *That a committee be appointed whose duty it shall be to enquire,*
>
> *1st. Whether under the different* [charters], *which have been granted by the State of Tennessee, they have the power to construct within the limits of the State of Tennessee, a direct Railroad route from Memphis to Clarksville, in direction of Russellville and Bowling Green in Kentucky.*
>
> *2nd. If there are charters granted by the State of Kentucky, for the purpose of constructing said Railroad from the Kentucky line in the direction of Russellville and Bowling Green.*
>
> *3rd. That said committee report such plan or plans, as will in their opinion prove the most efficient for the prosecution and completion of said Railroad.*

> 4th *If there has been a charter for a railroad from the city of Nashville, by way of Clarksville, to the town of Henderson on the Ohio river, in Kentucky, granted by the Legislature of Tennessee.*
>
> 5th. *If there has been a charter for a railroad from the city of Nashville, granted by the Legislature of Tennessee, to Memphis, and whether by the provisions of said charter a lateral branch of said road may be constructed to the town of Clarksville, and thence on to the Tennessee line, and that they also enquire at what point said lateral branch may, under provisions of said charter, intersect the proposed road from Nashville to Memphis. That they also enquire whether said lateral branch will be made.* [27]

The group returned the following day and answered questions that had been outlined in its resolutions a day earlier. Among its findings, they reported that Tennessee granted a charter, but Kentucky did not. This meant the MC&L officials would need to secure a charter from Kentucky.

The second day wound down and ended with a series of speeches. G.A. Henry gave a "spirited address, showing the importance of both the proposed routes to Clarksville, and urging the importance of a harmonious and concerted action on the part of the friends of both," as reported in the *Louisville Daily Courier*. [28]

The committee resolved, in part, that "a continuous line of railway from New Orleans, on the most direct route to Memphis, via Clarksville, Russellville, and Bowling Green to Louisville, and continued from Bowling Green to Danville, Lexington and Maysville, would give greater commercial facilities, traverse a richer section of country, and yield a better dividend than any railroad route now contemplated, and should enlist the united means and energies of the people along the entire route." [29]

On April 24, 1852, the *American Railroad Journal* reported that commissioners appointed for both the MC&L and the Memphis & Ohio, then still called the Nashville & Memphis, hire engineers to survey the route. The Memphis & Ohio was responsible for the section between the Mississippi and Tennessee Rivers, while the MC&L oversaw the segment between the Tennessee River and Clarksville. Delegates for a trio of counties in Kentucky—Todd, Logan and Warren—were tasked with surveying the route from Clarksville and Bowling Green.

According to the *American Railroad Journal* report, "The commissioners aforesaid to pay the engineers respectively employed by them out of the first

JOHN HURST & CO.

Historian William P. Titus included this view of Clarksville in his 1887 book, *Picturesque Clarksville, Past and Present. HathiTrust.*

money subscribed, either privately or by the counties, for the benefit of the railroad....That the delegates to this convention from the representative sections be hereby appointed committee to appoint speakers to canvass the region of country in the vicinity of the routes to be surveyed, and for the purpose of bringing the subject of these roads in all their bearings before the people."

The group wasted little time, and by the latter half of April had raised nearly enough funds, with the balance expected to be collected in short order. The *Louisville Daily Courier* reported: "The probability, therefore, is that within a few weeks, the Engineers will be at work laying out the route.

The Levee from Bluffs in Memphis, Tennessee, as shown on a postcard published by the Detroit Publishing Company. The city saw explosive growth in the mid-nineteenth century, expanding from fewer than 1,800 residents in 1840 to more than 22,000 residents in 1858. *New York Public Library.*

Our friends in the Interior counties may rely upon it that this project will be pushed with vigor and zeal. Men of energy, enterprise and capital have taken hold of it, and are determined to go ahead with it."[30]

On May 25, 1853, it "having been ascertained that a sufficient amount of stock had been subscribed under the charter of this company to authorize organization," commissioners appointed by the charter named a board of directors, as reported by the *Daily Picayune* of New Orleans.[31] In an 1880s history of the railroad, prominent Clarksville resident John W. Faxon wrote that the company secured $5,000 in investments.[32] At this time, the board named Joshua Cobb president of the railroad and elected T.W. Wisdom as secretary and W.P. Hume as treasurer.[33]

A decade after talk of a railroad "agitated" some members of the community, the MC&L finally had a management structure in place, though soon thereafter, some Clarksville residents feared the railroad would ultimately bypass the city.

A management team wasn't the only major breakthrough in 1853. That same year, a group of engineers—under the direction of Everett Peabody—completed a preliminary survey of the route.[34] Around this time, the MC&L sought financial aid from the L&N for the first time.[35]

Detroit Publishing Company published this image of riverboats on the Mississippi River in Memphis around 1906. *Library of Congress.*

On October 20, 1853, Montgomery County voters overwhelmingly agreed to subscribe $250,000 in tax dollars to the railroad. Of the 1,516 votes cast, 1,115 were in favor, while 431 were against the subscription. With the Montgomery County subscription, the railroad had $600,000 subscribed for construction.[36]

The *Louisville Daily Caller* proclaimed: "The vote was not as large as usual, but if all had voted, the majority would have been increased."[37]

Meanwhile, down the line, the Memphis & Ohio formally organized on October 4, 1853, naming Robertson Topp, a prominent Memphis lawyer who served in the Tennessee state legislature from 1835 to 1839, as president and John T. Trezevant as secretary.[38]

On May 26, 1854, J. Elder, W.H. Drane, Wm. M. Stewart, J.D. West, Geo. H. Warfield, J. Cobb, W. Broaddus, W.P. Hume, George T. Lewis and Tho. W Wisdom were named directors of the MC&L.[39] On June 3, 1854, Major G.A. Henry was elected president of the railroad. At the same time, Julius Adams was installed as chief engineer, and the business of determining the route was underway.

"We are now making our locating survey," Henry wrote in a note to the editors of the *Louisville Journal* in December 1854.[40] "It is our design to put this road under contract as soon as our survey is finished and we are put in possession of all the necessary estimates of the cost of construction."

A Push to Merge

On March 3, 1854, Tennessee lawmakers authorized the Memphis, Clarksville & Louisville to merge with the Nashville & Memphis and build a continuous line from Memphis through Clarksville to the Tennessee-Kentucky state line. Once merged, the new railroad would retain the Memphis, Clarksville & Louisville name. The state action also mandated that a majority of the railroad's board of directors reside in either Selby or Montgomery County.

Despite the action, the railroads did not merge and continued building separate lines. The initial track laid was a five-foot gauge, the same as that of the L&N and one of at least three different gauges found in the Confederate South.

The precise route was of particular interest to observers in Louisville and at points along the proposed road. A railroad between Louisville and Memphis had been a hot topic since at least 1851. While it certainly garnered ink in the newspapers of its potential terminal cities, it was also featured in headlines in important regional commercial centers such as New Orleans. Some in Louisville wanted an "air line"—the most direct route between two points—between their city and Memphis. However, such a line would pass through Dover, Tennessee, and Hopkinsville, Kentucky, completely bypassing Clarksville. While many in Louisville and Memphis might see no reason why the railroad had to pass through Clarksville, the prospect was unacceptable to power brokers in Clarksville.

According to newspaper reports, some naysayers of running the road through Clarksville questioned the route and the physical barriers it would have to overcome. In a note to the editors of the *Louisville Journal*, Henry said "any physical obstacle whatever may be made to give way if you have enough money to overcome it."[41] Money, however, was one thing the MC&L always found to be in short supply. Still, there was enough will—and capital—in Clarksville to see to it that the railroad would pass through the community.

A view of Louisville, Kentucky, published in the October 1854 issue of *Ladies' Repository*. The city grew from roughly 21,000 residents in 1840 to more than 68,000 residents in 1860. *New York Public Library*.

MC&L officials applied to the Kentucky legislature to continue its line from the state line to the L&N's route between its two namesake cities, but legislators apparently did not grant the application. G.A. Henry believed lawmakers exercised "intentional neglect" that led to the application's failure. In its wake, Henry found himself defending the MC&L in newspapers, particularly to Louisville business leaders. In December 1854, he said he waited to maintain his neutrality in a selection of the route, but he appeared to be trying to dissuade support of the air line, saying that building a road between Louisville and Paris was a "physical impossibility":

> *I therefore repeat, we do not here take any part in the conflict going on in your city between the advocates of the routes, for if either or both shall be built we are satisfied that Clarksville, possessing, as it does, great natural advantages and rapidly increasing in population, is situated directly on the "road to Byzantium."*
>
> *We will offer such inducements and solid arguments to Louisville that no other rival company can, inducements which, we are sure, will be mutually beneficial to her and us, and we do not doubt the choice she will make. We stand ready to embrace you at the State line, and to afford you a connection with the "father of waters" at Memphis. Will you meet us? Come on, then,*

in the spirit of friendly emulation, and three years will not have passed over our heads before we shall see the steam-car on the passage from Louisville to Memphis, as on the wings of the wind.[42]

The next month, Henry urged Memphis and Louisville leaders "not only to take us at our word but give us the benefit of their hearty co-operation and countenance." To be fair, there was probably no route between Louisville and Memphis that was free of all physical barriers. Henry argued that MC&L leaders were "willing to do the work and our hands ought not to be tied and our energies paralyzed by divided counsels at one end of the road or at the other." In his letter, Henry said:

The distance here between the Cumberland and Tennessee rivers is about 41 miles and we avail ourselves of the use of this distance to overcome the elevated ground known as the Tennessee ridge, [situated] between the two rivers, which we pass without a tunnel. It may well be doubted whether this can be done lower down, where the rivers approach within 10 or 15 miles of each other, without any perceptible decrease of elevation in the ridge between them. I state the fact as additional evidence that the route from Bowling Green via Clarksville is not impracticable, and that great injustice was perpetrated against us if such a report was made by Mr. Taylor to the Louisville and Nashville Railroad Company; that our road is now nearly located from the State line to Clarksville, 13 miles, 9 miles which are perfectly straight, at a low grade, and at an estimated cost of graduation, masonry, and bridges from the State line to the Cumberland river at Clarksville of $7,000 per mile. I am not speaking at random, but from the estimates of our engineer, who is locating with great care and exactness.—The cost of the same work from the Cumberland to the Tennessee river, a distance of 41 miles will not exceed $15,000 per mile. The cost of the bridges over the Cumberland and Tennessee rivers is not included.[43]

As it worked toward starting construction on its line, the MC&L's board elected William B. Munford as its new president on June 25, 1855.[44] Munford, a native of Danville, Kentucky, moved to Clarksville in 1839 and ensconced himself in many aspects of the community before his death on July 9, 1859.[45] Within a year of his appointment, he and fellow railroad officials had met with their colleagues at the Memphis & Nashville in Paris, Tennessee, to examine a consolidation of their roads. The discussion did not yield a merger.

Authorizing Construction

Once winter waned and spring started to blossom, on March 12, 1856, William Munford authorized the construction of the road between the state line and the Cumberland River.[46] By the end of April 1856, the railroad awarded a contract for the construction of the first thirty miles of the line to Champlain, Holman & Co. The *Clarksville Jeffersonian* reported that the road—"exclusive of the Bridges," rails and rolling stock—would cost $12,000 per mile.[47]

Although the railroad had a contractor, it did not have a finalized route. The company was mulling a pair of routes—so-called upper and lower routes. Residents living in the northern part of the city preferred the "lower" route, while residents in the southern portion of the city wanted the "upper" route.[48] In many ways, this spat sounds like an early version of modern-day NIMBY (Not In My BackYard) discussions.

Regardless, as long as the route remained unsettled, the location of a depot in town and where the road would cross the Cumberland River were also open to discussion. In its April 30, 1856 edition, the *Clarksville Jeffersonian* said the "interest of Clarksville should have a controlling influence in this matter," adding:

> But the question is an open one, and it is to be decided—now how is this decision to be made? We hope no individual will suffer his private interest or his personal preference to influence him. The enterprise is to mar or make our growing and prosperous city; to give to the whole county a new life, and develope [sic] resources hitherto unknown. Shall this great enterprize [sic] be warped into a mere machine to satiate the avarice of a few, or is it like a model government to be so managed as to the "greatest good to the greatest numbers."
>
> The interest of Clarksville should have a controlling influence in this matter; for as Clarksville improves so will the county improve, as she advances in population—in manufactures—in a word, in all that constitutes a thriving city, to that extent will she furnish a market for the raw products of the county, and afford facilities for developing its wealth and enterprize [sic].[49]

The difference between the two routes was a 10.0-mile-long section. The lower line contained a 1.75-mile stretch with a grade of sixty to sixty-eight feet and 8.25 miles of level grade. The upper line contained 7.0 miles with a grade of sixty to sixty-eight feet and 3 miles of level grade. The upper line would cost approximately $45,000 more.[50]

Railroad leaders responded with a notice in the May 14, 1856 edition of the *Clarksville Jeffersonian*, announcing a meeting on May 17, 1856, to discuss the routes and a meeting on May 24, 1856, to elect a new board of directors. The notice, signed by six people, stated: "We think the question too important to be decided unadvisedly, or by proxy."

When stockholders met "for the purpose of discussing the relative merits" of two routes under consideration, they agreed to abandon "the route below town" and agreed to submit "two up town routes" for stockholders to consider.[51] Proponents of the upper route used the neighboring community of New Providence—now part of the city of Clarksville—as a "bugbear" to frighten opponents away from building a bridge across the Cumberland River below the town.[52]

"Quite a number of engineers were consulted about the location, and all of them, with the [exception] of Mr. George B. Fleece, agreed that the upper route would not only be ruinous to the city, but would cause an unjustifiable expenditure of the means of the company," noted a later account of the railroad. "But Mr. Fleece calculated that the upper route would exceed in cost the lower by only $40,000. Upon Mr. Fleece's estimate, which proved to be accurate, the upper route was selected."[53]

Engineering firm Champlin, Holman & Co. published a notice in the June 11, 1856 edition of the *Clarksville Jeffersonian* asking contractors to submit sealed bids to work on the first thirty miles of the road, including clearing, masonry work, building trestles and laying crossties. The notice stated: "There is some heavy rock work, one Tunnel, a variety of earth work and heavy Masonry (with rock convenient) for the Cumberland and Red River Bridges."[54]

A subsequent notice in the June 18, 1856 edition of the *Clarksville Jeffersonian* read:

To Rail Road Contractors

Memphis, Clarksville and Louisville Railroad. The Board of the above Company [invites] bids for the construction of their Road from the Kentucky State line to the Cumberland River at Clarksville.

This Board will intersect at the Ky. State line, the branch of the Louisville and Nashville Road from Bowling Green Ky., and the Memphis and Ohio Road at the Tennessee river.

Other sections as well as the building of the bridge across the Cumberland river will be let hereafter. The Road will be let in sections of one or more miles to suit contractors.

Maps, Profiles and plans can be seen at the office of the Co., in Clarksville or enquiry made of the undersigned.,
W.B. Munford, Pres't.[55]

Just before the MC&L sought bids, in May 1856, the L&N started preliminary surveys for its portion of the Memphis Branch. The railroad examined three routes; two would branch off the main L&N line roughly a mile and three quarters south of Bowling Green, while the third would diverge at Franklin, Kentucky.

BREAKING GROUND

The Memphis, Clarksville & Louisville formally broke ground around 10:00 a.m. on June 23, 1856, in a spot some five miles from Clarksville proper. The ceremony featured speeches by MC&L president W.B. Munford and engineer George B. Fleece. As the *Clarksville Jeffersonian* noted, "the great enterprise, which for four years past has been the great and all-absorbing question among our people, is at last under way."[56]

As a part of the ceremony, Munford "threw the first shovel full of dirt, followed by the Directors, and Mr. Holman, the Contractor, and the Engineer," according to a report in the *Louisville Daily Courier*. "Thus this important work is fully commenced and it will be but a few months until the iron-horse will be panting over what is yet untouched ground."[57]

The *Clarksville Jeffersonian* stated: "The occasion was marked throughout by the most thorough and unmixed good feelings, and time after time the exulting shout as from men who had achieved a great victory would break upon the silence of the forest and reverberate through the vallies [*sic*] and about the hill tops."[58]

At pretty much every possible turn, newspapers reported that the railroad would be up and running in short order. However, their predications turned out to be overly sanguine.

While it had only been four years since the MC&L was chartered, in many ways, it must have felt like it took decades to arrive at this point. And while it might seem breaking ground was the peak hurdle facing the railroad, in reality, it was just the beginning; the next four years would be equally challenging.

In order to build the road, throngs of Irish Americans, such as "Patty" Sullivan, were instrumental. A newspaper article revealed that Patty Sullivan "secured a contract and opened the first cut between Clarksville and St. Bethlehem" in 1856.[59] The accomplishment was celebrated with a barbecue, a happening that was not entirely uncommon when workers accomplished key milestones during construction. Achievements were important on this railroad, which wound through hilly terrain and would require the construction of trestles, cuts and, ultimately, a tunnel near Palmyra, a small community located about eleven miles west of Clarksville along the Cumberland River.

Difficulties continued as the calendar turned from 1856 to 1857. Champlin, Holman & Co. was apparently dismissed. "We have heard but little about the rail road within the last few days, therefore we are not well posted, concerning the details of its progress, but presume it is progressing steadily," quipped the *Clarksville Jeffersonian*, adding that a number of workers arrived in the area and went to work on the tunnel in the Palmyra area.[60] The work was relet to smaller contractors, and by mid-February, work was "progressing as fast as could be expected," and 350 people were working on the road in the Clarksville area. The *Clarksville Jeffersonian* reported: "The road is now under the superintendence of new contractors, and bids fair [*sic*] to do much better in the future than it has in the past."[61]

Reading between the lines, one would assume work on the line was sluggish. Also slowing construction were "the delinquency of stockholders" and the railroad's inability to sell bonds. Some stockholders apparently claimed they were exempt from making payments because the railroad did not build its route precisely where they wanted.[62] In a May 19, 1857 circular to stockholders, president William B. Munford said:

> *The impetuous rampant energy of young America would rush forward rashly and involve the means of the company, whilst the over timid over cautious old fogies will ever cry out, a Lion is in the streets <u>beware</u>. Hence we are chided by some with being too tardy, whilst others predict that we are too hasty with our work, and should hold on and await the progress of other Roads and see what developments the future will make.*[63]

During the latter half of 1857, Tennessee lawmakers debated ending state aid to railroads, a move that might have spelled disaster for the MC&L and other railroads in the state. "More than half its means will be withdrawn and the enterprise will be effectually knocked in the head," the *Clarksville Jeffersonian* noted (in its typical overdramatic fashion).[64] The proposal, however, was unsuccessful, and work on the railroad trudged forward. However, the railroad apparently saw no need to submit a report for Tennessee railroad commissioner R.G. Payne's 1857 report:

> *The Memphis, Louisville and Clarksville Company have made no detailed report; but I will here state that thirty miles of their road is under contract and a heavy working force has been engaged along this section. This line when finished will give a direct connection between Memphis and Louisville, and thereby receive a large amount of through travel from betwixt Louisville and New Orleans and other intermediate points.* [65]

It is possible the railroad did not contribute a report because it suspended all contracts as a result of the Panic of 1857, [66] the first worldwide economic crisis.

In early 1858, the state opted to give to the MC&L two additional years to build the line. The action was met with excitement in Clarksville, where newspapers were always ready to trumpet good news about the railroad despite being a step out of touch with reality.

"We have been fortunate, indeed, in getting all we have asked for, and so much liberality, on the part of the State, ought to stimulate the Board to the to the full extent of its energies," the *Clarksville Chronicle* noted in its February 12, 1858 edition. The newspaper was confident two years would be more than sufficient time to complete the work.

"The grading of the portion of the road refered [*sic*] to, can be completed in perhaps, four months, and as Railroad iron is cheap and can be purchased on six months time, it occurs to us that it would be good policy to make the purchase at once."[67] Looking ahead, the *Clarksville Chronicle* knew the arrival of a locomotive would change hearts and minds, as noted in an article from February 12, 1858:

> *The whistle of a Locomotive will be a powerful appeal to the liberality of the public, and the confidence inspired thereby, can not fail to bring material aid to the enterprise; and we give it as an honest conviction, that the early completion of the road to the State line, will be worth thousands to the remainder, and, at the same time, arouse an active zeal in behalf of the branch road to Bowling-Green. We think, too. [sic] it may be demonstrated that the connection with the Nashville and Henderson road—opening a communication with the South—will furnish profitable employment to this short line of road, and be highly advantageous to Clarksville.* [68]

The Nashville community seemed less enthused. "This road, when completed, will no doubt be of great advantage to Clarksville," according to a report in the February 16, 1858 edition of the *Republican Banner*. Others were apparently even less optimistic, ridiculing the road as "beginning in the woods and ending in a hollow tree."[69] However, such derisions did not sway railroad officials.

On February 5, 1858, Tennessee state lawmakers approved an act to consolidate the MC&L and the Memphis & Ohio. If the boards of the railroads approved the consolidation, the route would have remained the same between Memphis and State Line.

A few weeks later, on February 27, 1858, Tennessee lawmakers approved an act to consolidate a portion of the MC&L and the Nashville & Northwestern Railroad to build "a common bridge across the Tennessee River." This would allow the two railroads to share construction costs. The *Clarksville Jeffersonian* opined that uniting "the means of the two companies for its construction, ensures the success of that section beyond a doubt."[70] The Nashville & Northwestern was chartered in 1852 to build a line connecting Nashville with the Mississippi River in Hickman, Kentucky, but by the time of the Civil War, the line only reached McKenzie, Tennessee, southwest of Paris, where the railroad interchanged with the Memphis & Ohio. The state gave the MC&L and the Nashville & Northwestern $100,000 each to build a bridge across the Tennessee River and $10,000 per mile "to iron the road."

According to the August 14, 1858 edition of the *American Railroad Journal*, MC&L and Memphis & Ohio officials "agreed on terms of consolidation." However, a state law required the companies to have sufficient funding to grade the entire line between Memphis and the Tennessee-Kentucky state line. Because the railroads did not have enough resources to cover an approximately twenty-four-mile-long section of the road between the Tennessee River and Paris, they did not consolidate.

The MC&L's annual report published in mid-1858 revealed $104,400 allocated for locomotives and rolling stock, with the total amount broken down as follows:

$45,000 for five locomotives
$2,400 for two baggage cars
$9,000 for four passenger cars
$32,000 for forty boxcars
$4,000 for ten gravel cars
$12,000 for twenty platform cars

However, the railroad did not have all the money its stockholders had agreed to provide. In a May 4, 1858 note to stockholders, MC&L treasurer Charles G. Smith urged stockholders to pay up and deliver their promised allocations:

> *I have the pleasure of announcing to you, that our Company have* [sic] *resolved to put our whole line of Road under contract, from the Kentucky State line to a point of connection with the Memphis & Ohio Railroad. We have just received intelligence from the President of the Memphis & Ohio Road that, that Road will be finished from Brownsville to the Mobile & Ohio Railroad, by the first of November next, and that it will be finished to Paris by December 1859. Our Road, to that point, will be under contract by the 1st July proximo, and in two years thereafter we hope to have the Road, completed.*
>
> *I therefore desire to say to the Stockholders, that I have had considerable difficulty in collecting the Stock calls due the Company, but hope to have no more. The Road cannot be built without money, and I earnestly appeal to you, to come forward and pay your calls. Heretofore, some have had doubts about the success of the Road. Now there can be none about it, provided you will sustain us. I intend calling on every Stockholder in the Road, within the next 25 days, and if they will each, make an effort and pay the amounts due, the work can be successfully carried on—otherwise its progress will be indefinitely postponed.*[71]

On June 26, 1858, the MC&L installed a new board of directors. Munford, in feeble health, declined to continue serving as president but did continue serving as a director alongside J.G. McKoin, Alfred Robb, R.M. House, William Broaddus, Jas. C. Johnson, G.A. Henry, W.A. Forbes, John K. Smith, Chas. M. Hiter, R.W. Humphreys, W.H. Drane, S.B. Seat and T.W. Wisdom.[72] The railroad selected William A. Quarles, a man history would better remember for his service in the Confederate army during the Civil War, to succeed Munford as the president of the MC&L.[73] Quarles was a staple of the Clarksville community. His family's history in the United States dated back to his ancestors who first came to Jamestown, Virginia. For his part, Quarles was admitted to the bar in 1848, ran for Congress in 1858 and later served as a circuit court judge.

Excitement for the railroad was building. "Our city is full of contractors from all parts of the county, who are bidding on the work yet to be let to contract," the *Clarksville Chronicle* reported. "There is but little doubt that

William Andrew Quarles (1825–1893) organized the Forty-Second Tennessee Infantry after the outbreak of the Civil War. He and his men were at the Battle of Fort Donelson in February 1862 and marched with John Bell Hood from Atlanta toward Nashville in 1864. He was a prisoner of war during the final year of the conflict. *Wikimedia Commons.*

the whole road will be under contract in a few days; and we understand that it is the intention of the new Board, to push the work forward with all possible speed."[74]

Still, not everyone was happy with the pace of work. In a piece published in the *Clarksville Chronicle* on October 22, 1858, Quarles aimed to tamp down some of the criticism aimed at the railroad:

We have already suffered much from the delay in commencing this link in the great chain of connection.—Our bonds have been sacrificed, our stock has depreciated, our credit has suffered under it, and our road has been ridiculed as one beginning in the woods and ending in a hollow tree; but we have been patient, wishing to pursue no other connection. —1st, because we believed it to our interests, and above all other considerations, we feel that our capital and energy should be so directed as to contribute to build up at least one great emporium of trade on the Ohio and in the limits of a slaveholding State; and it is not only a matter of policy but of good faith, that the different links should be completed as nearly simultaneously as possible, so that the proceeds of the road may become not only a means of paying accruing interest, but, I have no doubt in our case, a source of compensating dividend to the stockholders.[75]

"The Destiny of This Great Enterprise"

The railroad apparently found the right man in Quarles. After his appointment as president of the Memphis, Clarksville & Louisville, he placed the remainder of the road—slated to run between the Cumberland River in Clarksville and Paris—under contract.

Quarles wasted little time. On September 20, 1858, he "closed the contracts for the Iron and Locomotives for thirty miles of the road, the Iron to be delivered for the thirteen miles between Clarksville and the Kentucky line, by the 1ˢᵗ of April next," according to a report in the *Republican Banner*. "We learn that the contract is a very advantageous one to the company. Both the Iron and Locomotives were secured at quite a low figure."[76]

For his part, Quarles was well regarded in the press. "He has met and overcome difficulties in getting it to its present state of forwardness, that would have baffled many men who stand high as Presidents of Railroad Companies," read an article in the *Republican Banner*. "May he long live to enjoy the honors he has won."[77]

Even though MC&L engineer Gilbert C. Breed, who was elected Clarksville city engineer in January 1858, had resigned by November 1858 to form a business partnership with contractor A.J. Harrison, it didn't seem to stymie progress.

In 1858, The Louisville & Nashville Railroad's board decided to proceed with its portion of the Memphis branch. In November 1858, Louisville citizens voted to subscribe $300,000 (roughly $9.2 million in today's dollars) for the branch line between Bowling Green, Kentucky, and the Tennessee state line.[78] The citizens of Logan County, Kentucky, had voted in favor of a $300,000 subscription, prompting unbridled euphoria among railroad officials in Clarksville, who gathered to celebrate the news. MC&L president William A. Quarles noted "the destiny of this great enterprise now as fixed; that the great stumbling block heretofore in the way of its success…had been removed," as quoted in the *Clarksville Jeffersonian*.[79] Work on the sixty-four-mile Memphis Branch of the L&N formally began in 1859. Grading was completed on August 15, 1860, and the tracks were laid starting on September 16, 1860.

The optimism surrounding the railroad is perhaps best espoused in a rhyme published in the December 3, 1858 edition of the *Clarksville Chronicle*. Titled "The Iron Horse," the full rhyme included a number of racial slurs used at that time and indicated that the railroad would change the city's fortunes "and bring us back the cash we need to help our wives and daughters." The first three verses were as follows:

Soon we'll see him coming gleaming,
Then he'll make the welkin ring,
Rushing as he comes a screaming
Like the Eagle on the wing.

He'll bring our goods, and bring our coal
Nothing on the track he'll heed,
He'll rush us through from pole to pole,
As he flies with lightning speed.

He'll help to build our city up
Then we'll see its wealth increase,
While round and round we'll pass the cup,
With three cheers for Quarles & Fleece.

Another verse shared the writer's thoughts about the effect the railroad might have on the boats operating on the river:

The boats may then lay high and dry,
Or all be blown to pieces,
For swiftly on our horse we'll fly,
With speed that never ceases.

Although "speed that never ceases" might have been a bit of an overstatement, work on the MC&L plodded forward. By the latter half of March 1859, the first thirty miles were "rapidly approaching completion."[80] Crews were expecting to begin laying track by early to mid-April. G.A. Roth and Peter Fritz secured a contract for seventeen miles of crossties on the south side of the Cumberland River, "and from the character of these gentlemen the Company has every assurance that it will be speedily executed."[81]

But work on the railroad was treacherous business. This was readily apparent on April 9, 1859, when foreman Michael Cain was killed and two others were injured while working on a tunnel in Palmyra. As the *Clarksville Jeffersonian* noted on April 13, 1859:

A sad accident occurred at this Tunnel on the M. C. & L. R. R., on Saturday morning, the 9th inst, by which the foreman, Michael Cain, was instantly killed, and two other men badly wounded; having charged and fired the holes, one of them hung fire, and the foreman thinking it had missed, returned to fire it again; when within a few feet of it, the explosion took place, killing him instantly.

The deceased has left a worthy wife and two small children to sustain the loss thus unfortunately imposed upon them.[82]

Work on the railroad did not stop because of loss of life, particularly in the days before the existence of federal and state safety organizations and workplace regulations. By May 1859, grading between the state line and Clarksville was completed. The railroad received "two cargoes of Iron—one of 530 tons by the steamer Fort Wayne, and one of 350 tons by steamer Melrose."[83] A *Clarksville Chronicle* account noted:

Our readers are aware, we suppose, that this iron, although of the same shape as the old fashioned T Rail is hollow, and is claimed to be of better texture—"anti laminating," or less liable to "scale off" than the old iron. Besides this, it is a saving of 20 tons in the mile—the hollow rail requiring only 80 tons to the mile, while the solid requires 100 tons. The remainder of the iron we presume will be here shortly.[84]

The bridge over the Red River, to the northeast of Clarksville, was nearly finished "and when completed will, with the trestle-work attached to it, make one of the prettiest pictures in this part of the country."[85]

MONEY FOR NOTHING

Quarles was reelected as the Memphis, Clarksville & Louisville Railroad's president on June 28, 1859. The board consisted of a number of familiar names: G.A. Henry, A. Robb, H.S. Kimble, W.B. Munford, James C. Johnson, J.G. McKoin, George Stacker, T.W. Wisdom, W.A. Forbes, R.W. Humphreys, D.N. Kennedy, J.K. Smith, W.H. Drane and William Broaddus. The board also reelected Charles G. Smith as secretary and treasurer and George B. Fleece as chief engineer.

The railroad bridge over the Cumberland River, pictured here in March 2002, is one of the most recognizable landmarks in Clarksville. Some sources indicate the piers are the original pillars built before the Civil War. *Railfanning.org.*

A June 1859 report from MC&L treasurer Charles G. Smith revealed that the railroad had more than $1.5 million in assets, including $246,800 in individual subscriptions, $250,000 in Montgomery County subscriptions and $100,000 in subscriptions from the city of Clarksville. The state had appropriated $100,000 for the Cumberland River bridge, $100,000 for the Tennessee River bridge and $50,000 for the Red River bridge. The state also gave $560,000 for "iron and furniture for 56 miles" of the road.[86]

In the same report, MC&L president William A. Quarles defended the slow nature of construction. He admitted it was difficult for the railroad "to prevail upon stockholders to meet their calls." But, Quarles argued, the tide was turning, and anticipation of the coming of the railroad doubled the value of land along the line:

> *It is needless to recount the many obstacles the enterprise has had to encounter. When considered in its true position among the railways of the country as a great thoroughfare from Louisville to Memphis, we occupy the middle division, which it would manifestly have been unwise to construct any sooner than was necessary to be in a state of readiness to meet the Louisville*

Company on the one side, and the Memphis Company on the other. A railway without any connections beginning and ending in the woods, is of course profitless, and would have at once exhausted our principal, and left us to meet our interest account from a bankrupt Treasury. These delays, wise and prudential, as they are now admitted to have been, excited in the minds of many, a distrust in the ultimate success of the enterprise, and the impatient complaints of others.[87]

Building the physical road was no doubt a major portion of the work required to establish a railroad. However, that was just one element of the work needed to build an institution. Even as company officials were defending the pace of construction, the development of the railroad took a big step forward in May 1859. At that time, George B. Fleece, the railroad's chief engineer, traveled to Cincinnati "from whence he will ship the first Locomotive" to Clarksville.[88] The railroad's first locomotive, the Clarksville, arrived via steamboat on May 18, 1859.[89]

The 41,000-pound locomotive was intended for passenger service. "The Clarksville is a very pretty engine, but is built with more of an eye to *fact* than to *fancy*," boasted an article in the *Clarksville Chronicle*.[90] The steam engine was two tons lighter than the railroad's second locomotive, the Montgomery, which was intended for both passenger and freight service.[91]

The railroad finally had motive power. More and more, it was starting to look like a railroad. Now it just needed a completed route on which its trains could run. Slowly and steadily, the railroad was chugging along toward completion.

3

DISTURBING THE USUAL QUIET

In the decade before the Civil War, Clarksville was a quiet city. Firing up one of the railroad's locomotives caused a real sensation. On June 3, 1859, the *Clarksville Chronicle* reported:

> *The usual quiet of our Local sanctum was disturbed on Wednesday last by the unearthly snortings of the Iron-horse on our railroad. We immediately made telegraph time for the Depot, where we found the locomotive on the track, with tender attached, full of men and boys, all anxious to take a trip of two hundred yards, the length of the track at that time. The track-laying is going on well, and will soon be reaching out into the country. The Red river trestle will be complete on Monday next. The road commissioner will be here to-day to receive the Bridge already done.*[92]

The railroad took a major step forward about three months later, when passenger cars arrived in town. The *Clarksville Chronicle* reported on September 30, 1859:

> *We hail with pleasure, the arrival of a first and second class passenger Car for our Railroad. They were manufactured by Messrs. A. Street & Co., in Memphis, and their workmanship and general finish, reflect great credit upon that enterprising firm. They combine all the elements for comfort and safety in travelling, that are characteristic of Cars of similar grades upon the eastern roads.*

> *On to-morrow, there will be inaugurated a new era in the history of our flourishing city, for on that day a regular train of cars will commence running. When the fact becomes known to the travelling community, that we can leave here at early breakfast and reach Nashville in five hours after; we will expect to see full cars on each [successive] trip, and bright faces and happy hearts to join us in offering our warmest congratulations to the Company.*
>
> *The work on this side of the Tennessee River is progressing rapidly, indeed—beyond our most sanguine expectations. By the 15th of November, eight miles will be ready for the track, and we have received information from the most reliable sources, that ere the coming summer reaches us, the whole line from the Cumberland to the Tennessee River will be graded and in condition to receive the rails.*[93]

By now, the railroad had enough rolling stock and rail to begin operations. Though the complete line was far from finished, the MC&L Railroad's inaugural run was October 1, 1859. According to notices from chief engineer George B. Fleece—who, by then, was also apparently installed as the railroad's superintendent—and published in editions of the *Clarksville Chronicle,*

> *The Memphis, Clarksville and Louisville Railroad, will commence running on Saturday, the 1st of October, an Accommodation, Freight and Passenger Train from Clarksville to Tait's Station, (13 miles) near the junction with the Louisville and and [sic] Nashville Road, at the Kentucky State Line.… For the convenience of persons residing in the upper portion of the city, the trains will stop at a platform at Bradley's Brick Yard.*

By November 1859, the MC&L was operating a service to Nashville. The first train left Clarksville at 4:00 a.m. and ran to Tait's Station, located about a mile southwest of State Line. There, the train met "fine four-horse coaches," which took passengers to the terminus of the Edgefield & Kentucky Railroad, where they continued their journey to Nashville.[94] In 1852, the State of Tennessee chartered Edgefield & Kentucky to build from Nashville to the Tennessee-Kentucky state line, where it reached by 1859; the railroad later built to Hopkinsville and made up a part of the St. Louis & Southeastern Railway. The L&N subsequently subsumed the line, and it is now a part of CSX.

Any interest in the MC&L appeared to be short-lived. The railroad announced it would discontinue passenger trains—at least for a short while— after December 5, 1859, though it would still receive freight.[95] However, the looming threat of the railroad was still enough to worry steamboat operators. In January 1860, one proprietor announced reduced rates to "come in competition with the Railroads." The fare from Clarksville was six dollars to Louisville and eight dollars to Cincinnati. "These prices are lower than Passengers can travel on the Railroad, while we make no extra charge for Meals, and all people who travel with us acknowledge there is no comparison in the comfort."[96]

Across the Great Divide

While MC&L trains had started operations over a limited portion of the road, completing the route would require bridges over the Cumberland and Tennessee Rivers. By July 1858, a contract was in place for the Cumberland River bridge.[97] On October 22, 1858, the *Clarksville Chronicle* reported that contractors "have nearly completed the preparations for laying the foundation of the tower, and we hope they will get above the ordinary stage of the water before there is a rise to suspend operations."[98] That same day, the newspaper also reported "a call of 5 per cent on the capital stock" due on the first of November.[99]

Building the bridge would ultimately require six thousand yards of masonry for eight stone piers and would cost $103,000.[100] Companies working on the bridge included masonry contractor Maxwell, Saulpaw & Co.; McCallum, Seymour & Hawley, which developed the bridge; and Harrison and Breed, the company cofounded by former MC&L engineer Gilbert C. Breed.

In an advertisement in Henry V. Poor's 1860 publication, *History of the Railroads and Canals of the United States of America*, D.C. McCallum noted that the bridge "combines the principles of both Arch and Truss in so perfect a manner as to render their united strength available at the same time....While this Bridge is thus stronger and more rigid or inflexible, it at the same time requires less adjustment, and can be built of longer spans than any other plan of Trussed Bridge."[101] The *Clarksville Chronicle* described the bridge in great detail in its December 3, 1858 edition:

> *The masonry consists of eight distinct pieces. No. 1, a round pier, now started in the centre of the river, 28 feet in diameter and 70 feet high. 138 feet each way on the line of the road are piers No., 2 and 3 carried up to the same*

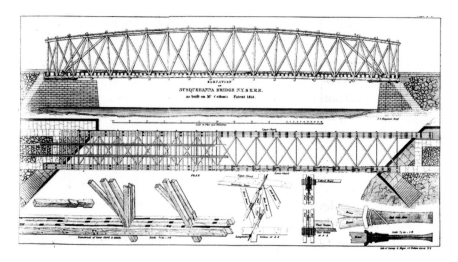

In the 1840s, Daniel Craig McCallum developed a truss bridge construction for railroad bridges. The McCallum inflexible arched truss, pictured here in an *American Railroad Journal* ad from June 19, 1852, was mainly built of pine timber. *Wikimedia Commons.*

height of No 1. No's. 4 and 5 are the same distance from the centre pier and the same height, and are situated up and down the river from the centre or pivot pier for the draw to rest on while it is open for boats to pass. No. 6 is at the edge of Parry's meadow 200 feet from No. 3, and No. 7 is the same distance from No. 2, setting on the river side of the road, or Water street. No. 8 will stand at the end of the present embankment. The track will run upon the top of the Bridge instead of through it, and passengers in looking out of the car windows, will seem to sail through the air while they travel from the crossing of the road, or this side of the river, till they strike the bluff beyond the Palmyra road, for immediately after crossing the Bridge proper, 2,100 feet or nearly a half mile of Trustle work, 30 feet high, joins the Bridge running to Parry's bluff. There will be about 6,000 yards of first class masonry— over a million feet of lumber, and at least 50 tons of iron in the Bridge.[102]

Work on the bridge continued, and by August 1859, the masonry for the bridge was "progressing finely, and will probably be finished by [the] 1st of January," the *Clarksville Chronicle* reported. "The superstructure cannot of course be put up till next summer, when the Trestle work of nearly half mile in length adjoining it will also be finished."[103] A pair of locomotives were already in service on the line, and passenger cars were expected shortly, according to the *Clarksville Chronicle* report.

Testing the Craftsmanship

Even as the bridge was under construction, its craftsmanship was tested. Riverboat captains were apparently upset at the prospect of a bridge passing over the river and potentially killing their livelihood. Many accounts indicate that riverboat captains routinely crashed into the piers, which were then under construction, in a bid to stop the work. Opponents of the railroad also placed obstacles in the way of the bridge, hoping to slow progress. The local press—particularly in Nashville—was more than happy to report on the latest mishaps.

When the water level of the river rose, it caused additional problems. In December 1859, at least four steamboats ran into the piers. On December 12, 1859, the *John Gault* "ran into the pier on this side of the river, and damaged her guards [the outer extensions of the boat] considerably." The next night, the *Scotland* "in moving up from the wharf to La Fayette Mill landing struck the upper middle pier, and, strange to say damaged the pier more than herself."[104] Apparently, "several of the heavy stones were loosened, and knocked out of position, while a slight injury to her guards was the only damage the boat sustained."[105] On December 19, the *Minnetonka* struck a bridge in Clarksville—presumably over the Cumberland River—and damaged "a portion of her guards and doing other injuries."[106] The next day, the *Tempest*, which was heading from Nashville to Cincinnati, "struck the pile of drift lodged against the upper rest pier, and was thrown over against one of the span piers," according to a report in the *Nashville Patriot*. "The force of the current carried her under the bridge, which took off her pilot house and chimneys."[107]

"We look daily to hear next of lives being lost, and suppose, too, this will be tolerated without a murmur," stated a report in the *Nashville Union and American*.[108] The following month, the railroad removed the debris from around the bridge piers.

Though some hoped the railroad would fade away, by 1860, eighteen miles between Paris and the Tennessee River were graded and ready for tracks, leaving a seven-mile section between Paris and the river that still needed grading. "The whole road will be in successful operation in a few months," reported the *Nashville Union and American*. "Many difficulties have been encountered in the construction of this road but all have been to a great extent surmounted."[109]

It would appear there was some level of consternation about the pace of construction. In February 1860, the MC&L's president and board of

Charles Oliver Faxon (1824–1870) was born in Catskill, New York, and after moving to Clarksville, he edited the *Clarksville Jeffersonian* newspaper. Historian William P. Titus later wrote, "He was, in fact, a walking encyclopedia, and could remember dates and speeches of the leaders of political parties almost word for word." *HathiTrust.*

directors announced they had "perfected for the more rapid prosecution of the entire line of the Road, and its early completion." On February 1, 1860, the *Clarksville Jeffersonian* reported a total of 2,000 men would be at work on the line between Clarksville and Paris within a month—an increase from the 1,200 to 1,500 working on the railroad.[110]

The railroad achieved a major connection when the Edgefield & Kentucky completed tracks between Nashville and the state line. A through train operated to Clarksville on February 15, 1860, for an event that included a celebration attended by a who's who of the community, including C.O. Faxon, editor of the *Clarksville Jeffersonian*; Gilbert C. Breed, secretary of the MC&L; and C.G. Smith, treasurer of the MC&L. The evening was capped off with a series of champagne toasts. The effects of the celebration were "distinctly perceptible" on the faces of "more than one of the enterprising and well-to-do denizens" the following evening.[111]

The direct rail connection was a vast improvement over the "fine four-horse coaches" that were transporting passengers between lines just a few months earlier. The railroad was a transformative enterprise for communities along the line and a true technological marvel. As noted in the *Clarksville Jeffersonian*, the train passing through the local community was a sight to behold: "The road appears to be doing a very satisfactory business and to be well managed. The locomotive with its long line of cars flying through the country, has not yet got to be a stale affair to the people living along the line, and men, women and children flock to the depots in large numbers to witness the wonder of the age."[112]

As the MC&L labored toward completion, the Memphis & Ohio was wrapping up construction. In early March 1860, the MC&L's board elected J.P. Ilsley as the new superintendent. A report in the *Republican Banner* stated: "From all we learn of this gentleman, the Board has made a wise selection. As a reliable business man, we presume [he] has but few superiors. From his long connection with railroad affairs, he will doubtless prove a great acquisition to the Company."[113]

On May 4, 1860, the first Memphis & Ohio train ran from Memphis to Paris, the soon-to-be terminus of the MC&L.[114] But the line running east from Paris to Clarksville, State Line and points beyond did not yet exist. This stretch of road included the vital bridges over the Tennessee and Cumberland Rivers. That same day, the Southern Express Company gave notice in the *Clarksville Chronicle* the company had made arrangements with the MC&L and the Edgefield & Kentucky for a daily express between Clarksville and Nashville. The Southern Express Company employed messengers to transport money, jewelry and other valuables in iron safes.[115]

By the end of May, the MC&L had received "quite a number of box and platform freight cars" that were manufactured in York, Pennsylvania, and transported via rail to Clarksville.[116]

Crashing Down

In May 1860, tragedy struck workers building the bridge over the Cumberland River. At least three men were killed when a temporary wire bridge (used to help in construction) fell. Nine men "were precipitated a distance of sixty-five feet into the water." Three men—Peter Flynn, William M'Dermott and Robert or William Douglass—drowned. A fourth man— Thomas Hennelly—had had both legs crushed; one was amputated. Another man, Edward Wells, leapt from the bridge and swam to safety, while another man, Ned Costello, was injured to a lesser extent and suffered "some severe internal injury." Three others—Michael Higgins, Michael Greeny and William Gorman—were unhurt in the collapse.[117]

After the tragedy, foreman Z.S. Main repaired the damaged wire bridge and returned it to its position across the river. A short time later, the bridge again fell into the river. This time, five men fell into the river; three—Main, Con. Hiland and P. McCallum, son of the inventor of the bridge under construction—were seriously injured.

"The fact that the foreman of the work and a son of the contractor were themselves engaged upon the bridge, and fell with it, must relieve the accident from any appearance of having been the result of carelessness," stated a report in the *Clarksville Jeffersonian*. "We are glad to learn that all who were injured by this last accident are doing better than could have been expected to-day."[118]

Another worker was injured in July when he "fell through the temporary flooring of the draw span, and went head first into the River, a distance of sixty feet below, uninjured. The wonder is that he did not strike some of the timbers of the scaffolding on his downward flight," reported the *Clarksville Jeffersonian*.[119]

Regardless, work on the bridge was reaching a conclusion, as this brief mention in the June 8, 1860 edition of the *Clarksville Chronicle* revealed: "The railroad bridge, across the Cumberland, having been completed, the first locomotive will cross over in a few days. The track-laying on the bridge and trestle work is progressing rapidly, and may be finished this week."[120]

Despite the challenges it was faced with during construction, the railroad expanded its locomotive roster when it added the W.B. Munford in July 1860, a steamer named in honor of its former president.[121] In an "unfortunate" twist, the locomotive Clarksville sank in the Cumberland River in June 1860.[122] The railroad was sending the locomotive via flatboat to Palmyra to "aid in the work there." Apparently, it was too heavy for the boat, and the locomotive "went to the bottom of the river."[123] One source indicates that the locomotive was recovered and leased to the Mississippi & Tennessee Railroad starting in 1862; it remained on that railroad for the rest of the Civil War.[124]

CAUSE FOR CELEBRATION

Work on the Cumberland River bridge was ostensibly completed near the end of July 1860. The *Clarksville Jeffersonian*, assuredly unbiased in its thinking, called the bridge "one of the finest Bridges in the country." The 692-foot-long bridge was "divided into two stationary and one draw span."[125] The hard work formally culminated in a moment of celebration on August 6, 1860, when the first train crossed the bridge over the Cumberland River.

The train eased out of the depot and made its way toward the bridge. People watched with "breathless interest," as if an impending tragedy was unavoidable. But there was no tragedy—only success. The *Clarksville Chronicle* reported on the historic moment:

> *It had become known during the day, that a train would pass over the bridge that evening, and by the time the evening train from Nashville arrived, a large number of our citizens had gathered at the depot to witness the event. Large numbers, too, congregated at the different points about the public square, from which the bridge could be seen, to witness the crossing.*
>
> *The fine new locomotive, W.B. Mumford [sic], in charge of Mr. Ben. Bartle, was the iron horse chosen first to tread this dizzy pathway. The locomotive and tender and one passenger car formed the train. About a dozen gentlemen, ambitious of being of the first party ever to cross the bridge, on a train of cars were mounted upon the engine and tender, and comprised the entire company. Hundreds of others were ambitious to be of the party, but were restrained by a fear that the bridge might not stand the test.*
>
> *A large flag was planted on the front of the engine; and, all else being ready, Conductor Cain gave the word and off the train moved. After getting under way, Capt. Cain took a position on the cow-catcher; and another gentleman of the party, during the entire trip, stood erect upon the little roof of the engine. On touching the bridge, Bartle set his whistle at a contralto pitch that never was heard before, and to this music steadily on we moved— with only here [and] there a little jolt, as if the noble bridge were trying to remind us of what it could do if it were to conclude to break down.*
>
> *But on we went—with flag flying, handkercheifs [sic] fluttering, and whistle shrieking—till the further side of the bridge was reached; and then one simultaneous shout from all on board, mingled with one wild shreek [sic] from the whistle, went up to announce our safe success; and this was answered by loud and prolonged cheers from those on the shore we had left. The test had been made! A train had passed over our beautiful bridge, and the noble structure bore the ponderous tread of the iron horse, without a strain or quiver!*[126]

Perhaps the *Clarksville Jeffersonian* summed up the situation best when it noted: "The bridge was tested, and the river had been crossed....The gentlemen connected with the railroad were very naturally elated at this triumph of human skill. They felt that the greatest obstacle in the way of the road south had been overcome, and that the road would now go on rapidly until it reached the Tennessee [River], each day increasing its length, usefulness and profits."[127]

With a major hurdle overcome, railroad officials found another reason to celebrate in September 1860, when they gathered to celebrate the completion of the railroad between Clarksville and Louisville. At about 2:00 p.m., city and railroad officials left Clarksville on a special train to Tait's Station. Attached to the end of the train was a flatcar with a six-pound brass cannon, "which as they left town, and at intervals along the road thundered forth its greeting to the coming guests."[128]

There, they met a second special train from Louisville with four passenger cars packed with dignitaries. MC&L president William A. Quarles began the event by welcoming attendees. L&N president James Guthrie then addressed the crowd. According to the *Clarksville Chronicle*, he "spoke of railroads as aiding to cement the bonds of National Union, by bringing people of different sections into closer intimacy with each other, and thus diffusing a feeling of common fraternity."[129]

James Guthrie (1792–1869) was secretary of the treasury under President Franklin Pierce before serving as president of the L&N. He later declined President Abraham Lincoln's offer to serve as secretary of war. *HathiTrust.*

"His speech, throughout, was very appropriate, but this part of it, where he spoke of the inestimable value and blessings of the Union, and the devotion we should feel to it;—of the efforts 'the politicians,' in some quarters, are making to overthrow it, and of the duty of all good citizens to oppose and resist them, was received by the multitude with loud and long applause."

The train then proceeded to Clarksville for further celebration. Major G.A. Henry addressed the crowd at one point, assuring guests "of the gratification it afforded the people of Clarksville thus to meet them, as neighbors—friends—brothers; thus to interchange fraternal sentiment, and strengthen the social ties that bind us together," the *Clarksville Chronicle* reported. "His speech was one that could not but be gratifying to our visitors for the earnest spirit of hospitality and goodwill that pervaded it."[130]

The railroad's arrival was unexpected for some, as evidenced by an unusual episode near Palmyra on October 16, 1860. According to a report in the October 19, 1860 edition of the *Clarksville Chronicle*, "a locomotive, driving a small train of boxcars, in coming to town from Palmyra" struck a mule. The boxcars derailed, and "in the momentary fright, occasioned by the accident, several persons jumped off the cars, and were right badly bruised, though none were seriously hurt." The mule, sadly, died in the collision.[131]

In the wake of the celebration, in October 1860, engineer Benjamin Bartle traveled to Philadelphia, "where he had been to receive a fine new locomotive just finished there for the Company." Bartle said "it is one of the best he ever saw (and he know the good ones, sure) combining great power with elegant finish." He "made one of the quickest trips home, 'on record,'" leaving Philadelphia at 11:00 p.m. on October 22, 1860; stopping in Cincinnati for nine hours; and returning to Clarksville at 7:00 p.m. on October 24, 1860. For its part, the "masheen"—which weighed four tons more than the W.B. Munford locomotive—arrived in Clarksville by way of Charleston, South Carolina.[132]

By the end of the month, the railroad was running two trains between Clarksville and Louisville. In its October 27, 1860 edition, the *American Railroad Journal* reprinted an article from the *Paris Sentinel*:

> *The grading on the Memphis, Clarksville and Louisville railroad, is now so nearly completed that they are receiving the iron rails, chairs, and spikes to commence the track-laying immediately at Paris, in the direction of* [Clarksville], *from which place the connection is made complete to Louisville. Between Paris and* [Clarksville], *the same road is now in running order, only a gap of about twenty-eight miles to be completed in the whole route. The road will be completed this winter, from Memphis to Louisville, and will be the best paying route in the union.*[133]

Even as the railroad ran limited operations, it was not a company that served everyone in the community. A notice from Superintendent J.P. Ilsley published in the November 21, 1860 edition of the *Clarksville Jeffersonian* reveals the harsh reality of the antebellum south for black residents:

> *Whereas, the President and Directors of the Louisville and Nashville Railroad, on the 1st day of August, 1860, passed the following resolution:*
> *"Resolved, That no person of color be taken in the cars for passage over any part of the Road or its Branches without the execution of an obligation signed by a responsible party or parties, to indemnify and save*

the company harmless for so doing." Therefore all parties will take notice that persons of color will not be taken on the cars of this company, for Points on the Louisville and Nashville Railroad, unless some person of responsibility known to the Agents of the Company, executes such an obligation as above required.

All persons of color wishing to go to and from Stations on the Memphis, Clarksville & Louisville Railroad must have Passes or permits from some person of responsibility, known to the Agents or Conductor of the company, and must be recognized by some equally responsible party as the person mentioned in the permit. All permits must state the Stations to which the [black passengers] desire to go and will be taken up by the Agent who furnishes the tickets for the trip.

Approaching Completion

Despite the euphoria surrounding the completion of this section of the railroad, it wasn't until 1861 that rails connected Memphis and State Line. The bridge over the Tennessee River was the last link completed on these three railroad lines.

Shortly after this celebration, Quarles resigned as the MC&L's president "on account of health and a pressure of other business engagements," the *Clarksville Jeffersonian* reported. "His services to this enterprise have been of [incalculable] value, and the Directors refused to accept his resignation until he made it peremptory."[134] To succeed Quarles, the board elected D.N. Kennedy, a native of Todd County, Kentucky, and a prominent banker in Clarksville, as its new president on October 30, 1860. Kennedy did not accept the position outright and asked for a few days to consider the offer. On November 5, 1860, he declined. Although he declined the role of president, he later served on the railroad's board of directors.

> *He had, he said, given the matter his most careful consideration, and had hoped that he might find it consistent with his private interests and engagements to accept; but had found that he could not do so. He felt highly gratified at the general desire manifested for him to take the position, and was anxious to serve the enterprise in any way he possibly could; but just now, when the interests of the road would require a great deal of the personal attention of the President, his own business would demand nearly the whole of his time.*[135]

The MC&L's board returned on November 12, 1860, and elected R.W. Humphreys as its new president.[136] Humphreys was an active member of the Tennessee community. In February 1860, for example, he was elected to the board of directors of the Branch Bank of Tennessee.[137] He was no stranger to the railroad. As the *Clarksville Chronicle* noted, Humphreys "has been in the Board a long time, and is familiar with the conditions and affairs of the Road, and will, no doubt, make a very energetic and efficient President."[138] Humphreys' tenure would be anything but a cakewalk as the country marched toward armed conflict.

In January 1861, Humphreys struck an agreement with W.F. Gray, a Dover resident and the mail contractor between Clarksville and Paris. The two agreed "to put a line of four Horse Stages in the gap between the Tennessee River and the end of the track, towards Paris, to run until the track-laying is finished to the Tennessee River." At the time, the gap in the track was only ten miles. Stages were scheduled to begin running January 21, 1861, and writers at the *Clarksville Jeffersonian* believed the completed line would be up and running by either March 1 or March 15: "The trip from Louisville to Memphis can then be made in from four to six hours less time than by any other route, and from this place in ten to twelve hours less time than by any other route. It will also be the quickest route from Nashville to Memphis."[139]

By the end of January 1861, a daily train was running between Clarksville and the Tennessee River, leaving the former at 4:00 p.m. Travelers presumably hopped a ferry to cross the Tennessee River, where they boarded the stagecoach to Paris.

Robert W. Humphreys (1824–1878), a Montgomery County native, was a prominent lawyer in Clarksville. *HathiTrust.*

By that time, the bridge over the Tennessee River was largely framed, with the exception of the "draw-span."[140] However, the span should have been completed and open for business five months earlier. By October 1860, the bridge was in "a very forward state," and its piers were built above the water line. It was expected to be completed by February 1861.[141] However, the piers were apparently constructed on insecure ground and had to be demolished and rebuilt, causing a delay in the opening of the bridge.[142]

Work on the railroad continued to be dangerous for many of the workers. It is not entirely clear how many people were killed, maimed or injured, as no such records seem to exist. Newspaper accounts provide the best insights into tragedies and mishaps that occurred during construction.

In one, James Richardson, an Irish laborer, was killed on February 18, 1861, while distributing telegraph poles to points along the track between Clarksville and Palmyra. According to a news account, he was knocked off a moving car while throwing a pole. The train ran over his legs, "mutilating them horribly."[143]

In another, according to a report in the January 25, 1861 edition of the *Clarksville Chronicle*:

Quite a dangerous accident occurred to the Louisville train, near the State line, as it was going out last Saturday. It seems that the "switch," where the accident occurred, had been properly [adjusted] *but not "locked"' and when the wheels of the locomotive ran upon it, the rails parted, and it ran off the track. Fortunately there were* [two] *freight-cars between the tender and passenger-cars, and their concussion with the locomotive and tender detached the passenger-cars, and they were left on the track. But for this the injury to passengers might have been very serious.—The locomotive was a good deal injured, and the fireman was so badly hurt that it was thought, for a while, he would die; but we are glad to hear that he is recovering. A passenger too, in the baggage car had his hand badly hurt, but no others were injured.*

These mishaps, presumably representative of many that occurred during the railroad's early days, did not stop the company from promoting its line. Around this same time, the railroad took thirty to forty people on an excursion to the bridge over the Tennessee River, which was nearing completion, in a bit of a public relations maneuver. "The country between the Cumberland and Tennessee Rivers, about forty-three miles in [length], is by no means an inviting one, though it contains much valuable and productive land, and vast quantities of excellent timber," reported the *Clarksville Jeffersonian*.[144] The newspaper account added:

The progress of the work upon the bridge piers is at present stopped by the extraordinary freshet in the river, but will be resumed as soon as the waters recede, which will doubtless be in two or three days. Several of the piers are finished, and are executed in Maxwell, [Saulpaw] *& Co's best style of masonry, which is about as much as could well be said in the way of praise. The timber is all on the ground, framed, and ready to go up as soon as the river falls.*

The track, which is being laid from Paris towards the river, is now within eight and a half miles of the bank, and is advancing at the rate of half a mile per day. Under no possible circumstances is it expected that the completion of the track will be deferred longer than the 15th of March, and the probabilities are that it will be finished at an earlier day. The day it is finished, there will be opened a new route from Louisville to Memphis, shorter than any other, and six or eight hours quicker in time. The bridge of course will not be finished as early as the track, but the company will put in a Steam Ferry, which will cause but a few moment's delay. [145]

The coming of the railroad also presented business opportunities for enterprising citizens. At the time, locomotives burned wood for fuel, and they needed ample supplies of it to operate. In January 1861, real estate agent T.D. Leonard advertised a pair of one-hundred-acre tracts of land near Cherry's Station for sale: "The land is good, and superbly timbered, a fortune to some man who wants to sell wood to the railroad, and have a nice little market farm left after taking the timber off." [146]

While the railroad may have suspended operations sometime in late 1860 or early 1861 "on account of the hard times," as the *Clarksville Chronicle* put it, trains were again up and running by February 1861—or even earlier, based on timetables printed in the local press. Perhaps Clarksville was a true railroad town for the first time, as trains departed Clarksville daily for Springfield, Nashville, Louisville and the Tennessee River. Plans for stagecoaches to complete the run between the Tennessee River and the Memphis & Ohio terminus in Paris were in the works. [147]

As the railroad prepared to commence operations, it started to fill open positions. In February 1861, J.H. Kean was appointed road master and placed in charge of a construction party between the Cumberland and Tennessee Rivers, "and the thoroughness with which he performed his work, commended him to the company as the proper person to be put in charge of the Road." [148]

W.W. Murphy was appointed conductor in March 1861. "The appointment is an excellent one, and Mr. M. is rapidly growing into favor with the traveling public," a *Clarksville Jeffersonian* article raved. "He has worked his way up from the position of brakeman to that of conductor, by strict attention to business, promptness and uniform urbanity, and we are gratified that his good conduct has been appreciated by the Company." [149] By early April, A.S. Livermore was appointed general ticket and freight agent— "a good office, worthily bestowed," the *Clarksville Jeffersonian* observed. [150]

By March 1861, post office officials had decided that the railroad would carry mail to and from cities between Clarksville and Paris as soon as the road was completed.[151] R.W. Humphreys and C.O. Faxon represented the MC&L at a meeting of railroad officials in Washington to arrange the schedule for the Great Southern Mail "so as to avoid the seceding States."[152] Tennessee voted in June 1861 to join the Confederate States of America—the last state to do so.

Under the agreement, the Baltimore & Ohio would transport mail to Cincinnati and Columbus, Ohio. The MC&L would help move mail to Memphis. "This is a very important arrangement, and will materially enhance the value of stock in our road," the *Clarksville Jeffersonian* predicted.[153]

Exuberance and Tragedy

As the calendar turned to spring, workers laid the final mile of track. In April 1861, newspapers heralded the start of trains running between Memphis and Louisville, and most reports indicate trains operating between Louisville and Memphis began running in April 1861. "Falling into the line of connected travel, we anticipate a large passenger business for the road from the day of its opening," heralded a *Clarksville Chronicle* report. "We are informed that the whole road will be in first class order by the day of opening, and doubt not that the connections will be regularly made to the entire satisfaction of the traveling public."[154]

Southbound trains were to leave Louisville at midnight and noon. The midnight train would reach Clarksville by 9:00 a.m. and Memphis by 9:00 p.m., while the noon train would reach Clarksville by 9:50 p.m. and Memphis by 9:30 a.m. Northbound trains would leave Memphis at 4:00 p.m. and 5:00 a.m. The afternoon train would reach Clarksville by 5:00 a.m. and Louisville at 1:30 p.m., while the morning train would reach Clarksville at 4:00 p.m. and Louisville at 11:20 p.m.

A new telegraph line, built under the direction of A.E. Trabue, to Clarksville from points north—including Bowling Green, Russellville and Louisville—was completed in January 1861. H.C. Cox was to take charge of the telegraph office in Clarksville.[155] The line extending south from Clarksville along the railroad's right-of-way was completed by May 1861, further closing the gap between cities in the region. However, conductor W.W. Murphy's "train beat the first dispatch," the *Clarksville Jeffersonian* humorously reported. "In fact, we are not sure that the dispatch has got along yet."[156]

GOING SOUTH.		
Leave—Louisville,	12 night.	12:00 M
Clarksville,	9:00 A M	9:50 P M
Humboldt,	4:30 P M	4:30 A M
Arrive—Memphis,	9:00 P M	9:30 A M
Leave—Nashville,	6:00 A M	6:30 P M
Arrive—Memphis,	9:00 P M	9:30 A M
GOING NORTH.		
Leave—Memphis,	4:00 P M	5:00 A M
Humboldt,	8:45 P M	8:45 A M
Clarksville,	5:00 A M	4:00 P M
Louisville,	1:30 P M	11:20 P M
Leave—Memphis,	4:00 P M	5:00 A M
Arrive—Nashville,	8:00 A M	7:00 P M

For the benefit of our readers, and others, we again publish the schedule of arrivals and departures of trains from this place to Louisville and Memphis, under the new arrangement, which takes effect on, and after next Monday, the 15th inst:

M. C. & L. RAILROAD.

Through to Tennessee River.

TRAINS run daily, Sundays excepted, for Louisville, Nashville, Springfield, and Tennessee river, as follows:

Leave Tennessee river for Nashville,	7:00, A. M
Returning, leave Clarksville for Tennessee river,	3:00, P. M.
Leave Springfield for Clarksville,	8:25, A. M.
Returning, Leave Clarksville for Springfield,	4:15, P. M.
Leave Clarksville for Louisville,	1:15, P. M.
Returning, reach Clarksville,	7:40, A. M.
Leave Clarksville for Nashville,	6:00, A. M.
Returning, reach Clarksville,	7:00, P. M.

GEO. B. FLEECE,
Ch. Eng. & Sup't.

Feb. 15, 1861—tf.

Left: The MC&L published this schedule for trains starting April 15, 1861; the journey between Louisville and Memphis took roughly twenty-one hours. *Library of Congress*.

Right: The MC&L published this notice in February 1861 to announce the start of trains to the Tennessee River. *Library of Congress*.

But the excitement that accompanied the railroad's achievements was tempered by tragedy. The railroad business of the mid-nineteenth century was a dangerous one, and the Memphis, Clarksville & Louisville was no different.

On May 1, 1861, two locomotives collided along a section of track between the Tennessee River and Paris. Two locomotives and two baggage cars were wrecked, but no one was hurt. "Both trains were out of time, but why they were out of time, or why they should run into each other, even if they were, we did not hear explained," the *Clarksville Jeffersonian* reported.[157]

A couple of weeks later, on May 17, the body of an enslaved man was found beneath the railroad bridge over Yellow Creek. His head and one leg were severed. "It is thought that he must have been on the bridge, either drunk or a sleep [*sic*] when the night train passed," according to the *Clarksville Jeffersonian*.[158]

ONE MORE RIVER TO CROSS

Despite the start of rail service, it wasn't until November 1861 that the bridge over the Tennessee River was completed. In fact, in March 1861, the *Clarksville Chronicle* reported that the railroad arranged a steam ferry boat "to

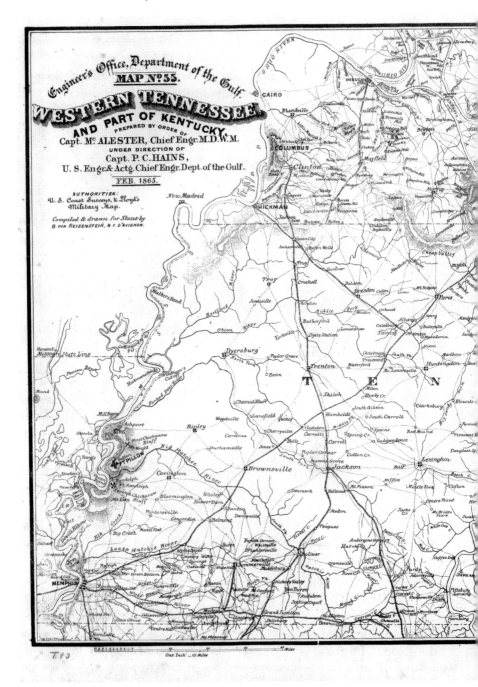

This February 1865 map shows the route of the MC&L. Memphis is located at lower left. Memphis Junction, where the L&N's Memphis Branch split from the main Louisville-to-Nashville line, is located toward the upper right, just south of Bowling Green. *Library of Congress.*

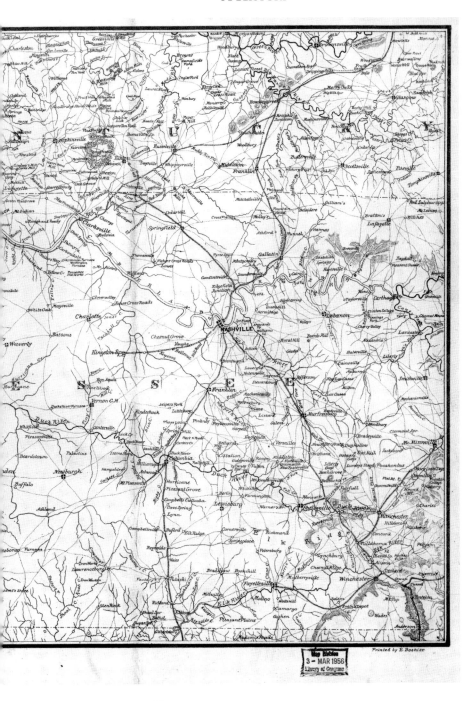

Printed by E. Boehler

Walter H. Drane, a native of Maryland, was a major donor to the MC&L. Historian William P. Titus later wrote that in "all matters of public enterprise he was among the foremost, and to his public spirit and energy the town of Clarksville was largely indebted for the building of her turnpikes, bridges and other enterprises that gave vigorous growth to the city." *HathiTrust*.

make the connection."[159] Regardless, the November 1861 completion of the Tennessee River bridge was as important as the earlier bridge crossing of the Cumberland River:

The railroad bridge, across [the] Tennessee river, is, at length, completed, and trains passed over it, for the first time, on Monday last. We congratulate our railroad company, and the business community generally, on this event. Especially would we congratulate the contractors upon the completion of a work, upon which they have labored so long, so faithfully, and under so many difficulties and disadvantages. There are not many contractors to be found, who would have continued, in times like these, and under so many difficulties, a work of such magnitude, with the faithfulness that Messrs. Maxwell, Saulpaw & Co. have pushed on this one. Accident, after accident, has befallen the work, involving months of delay, and the loss of thousands of dollars; State Bonds, which they agreed to receive, at par, in payment for the work, have been depreciated, by our political troubles, nearly fifty per cent, thus, alone leaving upon them a loss equivalent to nearly, or quite, half of their pay, and yet, in the face of all these difficulties and discouragements they have continued to prosecute the work with the same energy and alacrity, as if under the most favorable circumstances, and with a certainty of a large profit. Such faithfulness, in contractors, is, we regret to say, very rare, and when it is shown, cannot be too highly appreciated, and it is this that led us to say, in our last, that we should like to see our legislature take some action for their relief in this case.[160]

With the Memphis Branch of the L&N Railroad complete, through trains could travel directly from Memphis to Louisville. Unfortunately for the railroad, by the time the branch was completed, the Civil War was underway—an unfortunate turn of events for the railroads that resulted in a new set of challenges.

Building the railroad cost more than $2 million, and the railroad borrowed $1.582 million in bonds from the State of Tennessee.[161] Regardless, it was quite the accomplishment from an engineering sense, employing fifteen truss bridges measuring 2,255 feet in length, 7,676 feet of trestles and 119 culverts as it cut its way across the Middle Tennessee landscape.[162]

Completing the route would not have been possible if not for citizens, like Dr. Walter H. Drane, who gave money to the railroad's cause. Born in Montgomery County, Maryland, on November 1, 1798, Drane moved to Clarksville after graduating from medical school at Transylvania University in Kentucky. He paid $10,000 to help build the railroad. When he was later informed that his stock in the railroad was worthless and his money was gone, he simply replied: "It makes no difference; we have got the railroad."[163]

THE CIVIL WAR

O n April 12, 1861, the day the first shots of the Civil War were fired, the *Louisville Daily Courier* reported, "two trains will run daily each way between Louisville and Memphis, making the trip in eighteen hours. …The Memphis branch will open the quickest and most direct route to New Orleans, the time between Louisville and that city being reduced to some forty-two hours," the report stated. "The hours for starting from this point are not satisfactory to the people here, but we presume they were necessary in order to effect close connections with roads across the river."[164]

The paper also reported five conductors "now running on the trains from Louisville to Nashville will be transferred and run on through trains from Louisville to Clarksville." Conductors Sweeny, Taylor and Barry—"three as clever and gentlemanly officers as can be counted on any road"—were among the conductors assigned to the route. It seemed like everything was coming together for the railroad at precisely the wrong time.

Whatever normalcy the newspapers projected—and railroad operations exhibited—during the early days of the Civil War, a storm was brewing, and Middle Tennessee could not avoid its wrath. The war would soon wreak havoc on the Memphis, Clarksville & Louisville, just as it would so many other railroads across the Confederacy.

When the Confederates fired the first shots on Fort Sumter, South Carolina, the MC&L had four locomotives on its roster:

Clarksville (May 1859)
Montgomery (1859)
W.B. Munford (July 1860)
G.A. Henry (September 1860)

Compare that to the much larger Louisville & Nashville, which boasted dozens of locomotives operating across a total of 269 miles of track. That railroad had at least three different branches, including its portion of the Memphis line. As war broke out, the L&N would find itself in a precarious position as it served areas loyal to both the Union and the Confederacy.

Clarksville's location was unique in the Civil War. Tennessee was a Confederate state, while Kentucky, which was about ten miles north of downtown Clarksville, was a border state, meaning it technically fought with the Union. Similarly, the L&N was in a perilous position, as it passed through both Union and Confederate territory. The southern end of the line was sympathetic to the Confederacy, while the northern end was pro-Union. In Clarksville, residents were forced to make a momentous decision concerning loyalty to the Union.[165]

One challenge facing the railroad manifested itself in April or May 1861, when a federal official deemed MC&L tickets to be contraband. "Fearing that the tickets ordered by you…might be seized and confiscated under the order of the Secretary of the Treasury, we called upon the custom house

This builders' photograph depicts the G.A. Henry locomotive. Baldwin Locomotive Works built the steamer and delivered it to the MC&L in September 1860. *Railfanning.org.*

officer, and he decided very learnedly that printed tickets for a railroad company in a seceded State was an article contraband of war," a Northern ticket printer wrote to the railroad.

The *Clarksville Jeffersonian* was having none of it. "This is carrying the idea of contraband to an extremity. It is literally running the thing into the ground," read an article in the newspaper. "In the first place, the officer undertakes to decide, what, as yet at least, is not true that Tennessee is a seceded State, and then declares an article to be contraband of war, which every man who has brains enough to grease a gimlet, knows is not contraband."[166]

Despite the mounting challenges, railroad business continued. For example, the railroad advertised a meeting on July 8, 1861, to elect fifteen new directors to serve for the next twelve months.[167] The railroad's stockholders named R.W. Humphreys, John K. Smith, Alfred Robb, G.A. Henry, D.N. Kennedy, William A. Quarles, George Stacker, Joshua Elder, John F. House, George H. Warfield, Larkin Bradley, W.H. Drane, Thomas McCulloch, William Broaddus and Thomas J. Pritchett as the new directors.[168]

The impending war initially had a positive effect on the railroad, and travel on it was heavy, thanks in part to people avoiding travel via steamboats, particularly in and around Cairo, Kentucky. On May 3, 1861, the *Clarksville Chronicle* reported:

> *The passenger business of the Railroad from Memphis to Louisville is now very large. The* [interference] *of Lincoln's minions at different points, but particularly at Cairo, with the steamboats, has diverted travel from the river to the railroad; and the route from Memphis via Clarksville being the shortest and quickest from all points South, is bound to absorb nearly all the travel.—One evening this week the train from Memphis brought to this place 175 passengers, 124 of these being through passengers.*
>
> *Mr. Cain and Mr. Murphey* [sic] *are the Conductors on our division of the Road; and more efficient and accommodating officers can't be "dug up" anywhere.*[169]

Operations, however, did not always go off without a hitch. On July 5, 1861, an Edgefield & Kentucky train arrived at State Line. The train's conductor asked all passengers traveling to Louisville to ride in one car and all passengers headed to Memphis to ride in another. When the train reached the junction at State Line, the conductors apparently attached the Louisville car to the proper train but failed to attach the Memphis-bound coach—and its passengers—to the train, "leaving all of said passengers all night to shift as best they could in the woods," as there was no hotel in the area at the time. Meanwhile, the train's conductor and the railroad's superintendent shuffled off toward Clarksville.[170]

Railroad officials had bigger matters preoccupying their minds, as the march to war in Clarksville soon began in earnest. In June 1861, Montgomery County citizens cast 2,631 votes for separation and 33 against.[171] There weren't any "meaningful" battles in Clarksville, nor were there any events that helped shape the outcome of the conflict. Nonetheless, troops on both sides recognized the strategic importance of Clarksville and the MC&L.

As expected during such a conflict, residents experienced railroad delays as connections to the north were eliminated, which happened starting in July 1861.[172] In the war's first months, the railroad allowed troops serving Tennessee or the Confederacy to ride its rails for free. According to a July 1861 "Notice to Military Companies" from George B. Fleece, the MC&L superintendent, which was published in the *Clarksville Jeffersonian*:

> *Military Companies, or individual members of Military Companies, in the service of the State of Tennessee, or of the Southern Confederacy, will pass free on this road under the following restrictions.*
>
> *1st. Military Companies to pass free must, when practicable, obtain a free pass for the Company from the Superintendent—or, when this is impracticable, must travel under command of some officer of their Company, whose statement to the Conductor that his Company are moving under orders, on military duty, will insure the Company a free pass.*
>
> *2d. Individual members of such Companies, must obtain a pass from the Superintendent, which will always be granted on a statement of the Captain of their respective Companies, that they are members thereof, and are traveling under orders on military duty.*[173]

Despite the state of war, the business of running a railroad continued— sometimes with seemingly little interruption. On July 8, 1861, shareholders elected a slate of directors: R.W. Humphreys, John K. Smith, William A. Quarles, George Stacker, Joshua Elder, John F. House, George H. Warfield, Larkin Bradley, W.H. Drane, Thomas McCulloch, William Broaddus and Thos. J. Pritchett.[174]

By July 26, 1861, the *Clarksville Chronicle* reported that there was "only one train a day, now, to and from Louisville," operating over the roughly thirteen-mile stretch of the MC&L between Clarksville and State Line, with the remainder traveling over the L&N. It departed Clarksville at 6:00 a.m. and arrived at 7:00 p.m.[175]

However, starting September 25, 1861, the railroad announced a new schedule. Passenger trains ran daily, with southbound accommodation trains—a local train that made every stop along the line—on Monday, Wednesday and Friday. Northbound accommodation trains ran on Tuesday, Thursday and Saturday. In September 1861, southbound passengers would:

Leave Bowling Green at 3:20 p.m.
Leave Russellville at 5:15 p.m.
Leave State Line at 7:00 p.m.
Leave Clarksville at 7:40 p.m.
Arrive at the Tennessee River at 10:30 p.m.

Meanwhile, northbound trains would:

Leave the Tennessee River at 3:00 a.m.
Leave Clarksville at 5:40 a.m.
Leave State Line at 7:00 a.m.
Leave Russellville at 8:17 a.m.
Arrive at Bowling Green at 10:10 a.m.[176]

On September 13, 1861, the *Clarksville Chronicle* reported that Fleece was "infusing more perfect system and order, in its conduct and management, than have heretofore obtained, and doing everything he can, to develope [*sic*] its fullest use to the public and its best paying capacities to stockholders."[177] In that same issue, the newspaper published the constitution of the Confederate States of America. Even if the railroad had not yet felt its effects, war was on the horizon. The following week, the newspaper reported the Soldiers' Aid Society shipped via railroad "about 20 large boxes, filled with winter clothing, for our boys in Virginia."

War Comes to Middle Tennessee

By October, railroad travel between Clarksville and Bowling Green was decreasing. About this time, Confederate general Simon Bolivar Buckner proposed to L&N president James Guthrie that the railroad be allowed to continue running trains. Bolivar indicated he would appoint his own agents to operate trains over the line in areas he controlled if Guthrie did not agree.

On the evening of October 19, 1861, the bridge across Budds Creek (sometimes spelled Budd's Creek) was damaged, but the precise cause is something of a mystery, as the *Clarksville Jeffersonian* reported two different happenings at the bridge on the same day.

In one report, the newspaper said a twenty-five-car train transporting soldiers derailed near the Budds Creek crossing after striking a "large log" placed across the tracks. "The villains who commit such outrages, as this, should be [ferreted] out and brought to summary punishment," the *Clarksville Jeffersonian* declared.[178] While it is hard to say whether pro-Union forces carried out this act, it signaled the start of years of sabotage against the railroad.

In a second account, the newspaper reported the bridge burned in three places, and it did not hesitate to assign blame. "It was undoubtedly the work of some Lincoln incendiary," the *Clarksville Jeffersonian* claimed. "Our military authorities cannot be too vigilant in the protection of our Railroad and river. Let guards be stationed at each bridge, as has been done in East Tennessee, for we have almost as much to fear as the Railroad Co's., in that division of the State."[179]

A train heading from Memphis apparently discovered the burned bridge and opted not to attempt the crossing, calling for a second train to continue the journey north toward Clarksville. Another account indicated local residents discovered the blaze and quickly extinguished it.

Regardless, while initial reports indicated the bridge was a total loss, it was "little injured." Workers repaired the crossing and returned it to service in quick order.[180] Subsequent accounts indicate the burning was accidental.[181]

At some point, Fleece was appointed superintendent of the railroad line between Bowling Green and Paris, a section that included the MC&L and the L&N's portion of the Memphis Branch. Fleece later assumed responsibility for the portion of the L&N line between Bowling Green and Nashville. In October 1861, Fleece appointed G.C. Breed as master of transportation and assistant superintendent in Bowling Green. The looming war presented another problem, as the MC&L and other railroads in Tennessee were falling behind on their interest payments.

Elsewhere along the line, workers struggled to complete the bridge across the Tennessee River. Work was slowed by numerous mishaps, including "several serious accidents." In one, workers had to rebuild a bridge pier. In another, a span fell. That is "to say nothing of lesser misfortunes" apparently

A solider guards a railroad bridge at Strawberry Plains, located twenty miles northeast of Knoxville, Tennessee. Railroad infrastructure—specifically, bridges—became a key target of military action during the Civil War. *Library of Congress.*

not worthy of ink in the *Clarksville Chronicle*. In many ways, the bridge was symbolic of the hope the paper's editors held for the new Confederate States of America:

> *The importance and value of this line of railway, we do not believe, have ever yet been properly estimated—nor will they ever be, until when, after peace has been restored, the great energies of our new republic shall have been brought into full exercise, and the teeming plenty of our soil, and the fruits of our new-born mechanical industry, begin to find their way to the markets of the world, over Southern roads, and through Southern ports, instead of being tributary, as heretofore, to the plethoric and arrogant commercial supremacy of the North.*[182]

Railroad bridges were easy targets for guerrillas. Bridges across the Confederate states were burned, and newspapers featured the latest news about burned bridges. So important were railroads that the Tennessee legislature passed a measure exempting telegraph operators and necessary railroad employees from serving in the state militia.

The coming fight did nothing to improve safety, and December 1861 seemed to be a particularly deadly month for the railroad. On December 19, the trucks on an express car on the fast-running train from Memphis broke, sending a pair of wheels "flying off." Somehow, the "coupling held up the end of the car until the train was stopped."[183]

On the morning of December 31, an unidentified soldier fighting for a Mississippi regiment died after he fell from a train as it ran near Cumberland City. That evening, two soldiers—one belonging to the Tenth Arkansas regiment and the other to a Mississippi regiment—stepped off the train while it was stopped on a bridge in Clarksville (presumably an approach to the Cumberland River bridge). The men fell to the ground forty feet below; one died instantly, and the other was badly injured, presumably fatally. In an odd twist of fate, a few moments later, while the train was still making its way across the bridge, two other soldiers stepped out of the cars and fell through the bridge to the ground forty or fifty feet below. Miraculously, they escaped serious injuries. The following day, a soldier named M.C. Turner from Corinth, Mississippi, was found lying across the railroad "cut nearly in two, and horribly mangled," the *Clarksville Jeffersonian* reported, providing rather gruesome details. He likely fell between the train's cars.[184]

The War's First Full Year

Even as the War Between the States moved into its first full year, in some aspects, life continued as usual in many ways. Local government officials continued to collect railroad taxes to pay for the Memphis, Clarksville & Louisville, but the tone of local newspapers illuminated the changing situation. An advertisement seeking fifty thousand bushels of corn from the Clarksville region to send to Confederate troops appeared in print several times.

In some ways, one of the first—and perhaps most tangible—impacts the Civil War had on Middle Tennessee was increased rail traffic. In a January 2, 1862 letter to Major A.J. Smith, MC&L superintendent George

B. Fleece said the railroad had 175 total cars—120 boxcars and 55 flat cars—owned by either the MC&L or the L&N's Memphis Branch. This equipment allowed for:

- A train daily northward from Bowling Green, capable of moving ten carloads of corn
- A freight train daily each way between Nashville and Bowling Green, carrying twelve cars each way
- A freight train daily between Paris and Bowling Green with twelve cars
- A passenger train each way on the main stem and the Memphis Branch

"This is the maximum capacity of the roads. Should there be any extraordinary demand upon both stems at the same time, both will require help from other roads," Fleece said. "If made on one stem, the regular business of the other must stop to meet it." At "every station there is a large accumulation of freight, consisting of hogs, corn, flour, &c," Fleece noted. "The passenger travel is also large. In addition to all, troops move in great numbers. In a word, the entire road is crowded with business to an extent unprecedented in the history of any branch of it."[185]

Fleece also noted:

> I suggest that the superintendent may be allowed to establish a schedule best adapted for the speedy, safe, and certain final accomplishment of all work, and that the public shall be notified that this schedule shall remain undisturbed, save under the requisition of some one officer of the army, or that a requisition shall be made upon other roads for the amount of machinery required to meet the business.
>
> Should this course be adopted, the funds now in hands, the earnings of the main stem and branch, will pay a large proportion of the value of machinery required, and perhaps the Memphis, Clarksville and Louisville Railroad Company would make an advance sufficient to pay the balance. This property might—would largely increase the earnings of the road, and at the same time meet the difficulties before us. I know of no remedy better than the last suggested, but without this the first plan suggested is the only one under which I can promise to do justice to the army, the stockholders, or myself.[186]

Around this time, General Albert Sidney Johnston appointed George B. Fleece the superintendent of the L&N. The appointment was heralded in the local newspaper:

This appointment is very honorable to Mr. Fleece, since it was tendered to him, by Gen. Johnston, from the latter's observation of Mr. F's. excellent management of the road from here to Bowling Green. He was highly complimented thereupon, when he received the latter appointment, and very justly too, for there are but few men who under the difficulties and perplexities of the past six months, could have managed the road so successfully and satisfactorily as he has done.[187]

Fearing a Union attack, Confederate troops in the area bolstered defenses at Fort Donelson in Dover, Tennessee, and Fort Henry, named in honor of G.A. Henry and located on the Kentucky-Tennessee line west of Dover. In November 1961, Confederate troops also built Fort Defiance, which overlooked the convergence of the Cumberland and Red Rivers in Clarksville. The importance of Confederate troops' preparations was not lost on eagle-eyed observers, including newspaper editors.

"The capture of these Forts would give [Union troops] the control of the Memphis, Clarksville & Louisville Railroad, and expose our troops in Kentucky to an attack in the rear, and afford the enemy an admirable chance for a flank movement against our army on the Mississippi," the *Republican Banner* reported on November 2, 1861.[188]

Federal transport ships sit docked along the banks of the Tennessee River during the Civil War. *Library of Congress.*

Their fears were right: Vital infrastructure elements, including the MC&L, were in the proverbial crosshairs of Union leaders, who knew disabling the line and its corresponding telegraph link would be necessary. "It will be of the first importance to break the railroad communications, and, if possible, that should be done by columns moving rapidly to the bridges over the Cumberland and Tennessee," noted Brigadier General Don Carlos Buell, speaking to the strength of Confederate forces in the area.[189]

Buell certainly recognized the importance of railroads. In March 1862, he authorized James J. Andrews to conduct a mission to steal a locomotive in Atlanta and destroy the Western & Atlantic Railroad between Atlanta and Chattanooga, Tennessee. The mission was aborted when Andrews failed to connect with a locomotive engineer. Andrews returned a month later to carry out the ill-fated Andrews Raid (or Great Locomotive Chase).

On February 7, 1862, a landslide east of the Tennessee River caused considerable damage to the railroad. However, this paled in comparison with what was to come. Accounts indicated it would take days to repair the tracks and return them to running order. Elsewhere, on the L&N's

In November 1861, Confederate troops built defenses overlooking the Cumberland and Red Rivers. Following a major battle at Fort Donelson in nearby Dover, Confederate troops abandoned Clarksville; Union troops later found the abandoned fort and reworked it for their needs. In 2011, the city opened a $2 million interpretive center to tell the story of Fort Defiance, pictured here in 2012. *Railfanning.org.*

Union brigadier general Don Carlos Buell recognized the importance of railroads. He authorized a Union spy to travel behind enemy lines to Atlanta and steal a locomotive with the intent of destroying rail lines and ordered troops to destroy railroad bridges in Middle Tennessee. *Library of Congress.*

Memphis Branch, in early February, Union troops destroyed the bridge over Whippoorwill Creek in Logan County, Kentucky, but it was quickly restored to service.

The real forerunner of the looming devastation came on February 8, 1862. On that day, Major General Henry Wager Halleck wrote to Brigadier General Ulysses S. Grant: "If possible, destroy the bridge at Clarksville. It is of vital importance, and should be attempted at all hazards."[190] At this point, the MC&L's bridges were on borrowed time.

Despite the Confederate measures to build defenses in the region, Union troops advanced, and Forts Donelson, Henry and Defiance soon fell to Union troops.[191] Following the major battle at Fort Donelson in February 1862, Confederate soldiers abandoned Clarksville. Union troops later found the abandoned Fort Defiance, perched two hundred feet above the rivers' confluence, and reworked it for their needs.

Railroad trestles, especially, took a hit during the Civil War when invading Union forces destroyed the wooden structures. There are several recorded raids intended to destroy bridges, and both sides had the railroad in their sights. A February 8, 1862 message from William W. Mackall, assistant adjunct-general for the Confederate States of America, probably best sums up the approach: "Destroy every bridge and trestle on the railroad from Tennessee Crossing to Paris." Union troops obliged and destroyed tracks at the Tennessee River crossing.

Union general Henry W. Halleck in a photo taken between 1860 and 1865. He ordered troops to destroy bridges in Clarksville. *Library of Congress.*

"But a result of this great victory is a cutting off of the main channel of rebel communication East and West. Already our forces have destroyed the tressle-work [*sic*] approaching the bridge of the Memphis, Clarksville and Louisville Railroad," Union general Henry W. Halleck noted.[192] After the fall of Fort Henry and Fort Donelson, the North no longer needed the railroad for transportation. Tracks passing through the area fell into a state of disrepair and were sparingly used—if they were used at all.[193]

That same month, Confederate troops "set fire, against the remonstrances of the citizens, to the splendid railroad bridge across the Cumberland River," according to A.H. Foote, flag officer, Commanding Naval Forces, Western Waters.[194]

"On the approach of the gunboats, the railroad bridges over the Cumberland and Red Rivers were set on fire, and that [the one over the] Red River is destroyed. The other is but little damaged," stated a *New York Times* report on February 23, 1862.[195]

Foote arrived in Clarksville on February 19. Much of the population had already fled the city. "In short, the city was in a state of the wildest commotion from rumors that we would not respect the citizens either in their persons or in their property. I assured those gentlemen that we came not to destroy anything but forts, military stores, and army equipments," Foote wrote.[196] City leaders—including Cave Johnson, Mayor George Smith and Judge Thomas Wisdom—met with Foote, and Clarksville surrendered.

This fighting hindered the railroad's ability to turn a profit, and by April 1862, it had twice defaulted on paying the interest on its bonds. MC&L president Robert W. Humphreys probably did not help the cause when he apparently dismissed superintendent Gilbert C. Breed for his pro-Union sentiments.

Andrew Johnson served as military governor of Tennessee from March 12, 1862, to March 4, 1865, when he was inaugurated as vice president of the United States. *Library of Congress.*

That action prompted the Connecticut-born Breed to write to Andrew Johnson, then military governor of Tennessee, on April 12, 1862—the same day James J. Andrews and a group of Union spies stole a locomotive in Big Shanty (Kennesaw), Georgia, with the goal of destroying a different Confederate railroad, the Western & Atlantic. Breed inquired "whether the State should not take charge of its own for the benefit of the people—rather than that loud mouthed secessionists should still longer oppress those who would like to open the channels of business, and those who were the laborers and Employees on this and other connecting roads."[197]

By April 1862, some MC&L stockholders reached out to L&N management. They hoped the L&N would operate at least a portion of the MC&L.

On April 28, 1862, the L&N board agreed to operate the MC&L from the state line to the Red River (about three miles east of Clarksville) until the bridge over the Red River was repaired and trains could continue to travel into Clarksville proper. In a May 3, 1862 letter, L&N president James Guthrie indicated the railroad planned to build a depot and a turntable at the Red River terminus.[198]

The L&N operated the MC&L from the Tennessee-Kentucky state line to Clarksville for the remainder of the war.

SOME TRAINS RUN

Newspaper accounts of Civil War activity in the area are unreliable. Regardless of the fighting, portions of railroads remained in service. Confederates burned a trestle near Hampton's Station, situated about three miles southwest of the state line and about ten miles from Clarksville. Louisville & Nashville workers repaired the trestle, but guerrillas burned it again in late May 1863.[199]

However, the L&N reestablished through service between its two namesake cities on February 1, 1863. On July 1, 1863, the same day the Battle of Gettysburg began, service between Louisville and Clarksville returned after L&N workers repaired the trestle over the Red River.[200] On December 5, 1863, the *American Railroad Journal* reported that the L&N "agreed to operate the 14 miles of the Memphis, Clarksville and Louisville Railroad, between the State line and Clarksville, and to divide the profits after paying cost of operating. The rebel raids and unsafe condition of the country prevented the operation, except for a few months." The gross earnings of the railroad, operating over fourteen miles, for the three months ending in June 1863 were $554.23, while the cost of operating and rebuilding the Red River bridge was $6,811.89.

Perhaps more than ever, the railroad was a connection to the outside world. Nowhere was that more apparent than at Tait's Station, a small community about a mile from State Line. At 4:00 p.m. every day, residents would gather at the station there to wait for the train, which brought newspapers. "On these occasions national affairs are ventillated [*sic*] in every form of discussion, and sapient indeed are some of the theories set forth," said a report in the *Clarksville Gazette*.[201]

Tait's Station was home to warehouses, a tobacco "stemmery," a hotel, a brickyard and three residences. The hotel offered coffee, rolls, biscuits, egg-bread, waffles, broiled chicken, fried ham, hash, sausage and boiled eggs to weary travelers. "Everything too, is neat, clean and well cooked, showing the management and supervision of a skilled housekeeper," a letter-writer noted in an account published in February 1864 in the *Clarksville Gazette*. The "amount of business [that] is done here…would astonish you."[202]

In August 1864, the U.S. Military Railroads repaired and opened the sixty-two-mile long Nashville & Clarksville Railroad, consisting of forty-seven miles of the Edgefield & Kentucky (between Nashville and the Tennessee-Kentucky state line) and fifteen miles of the MC&L (between State Line and Clarksville). In December 1864, Confederate forces with General Hylan B. Lyon again destroyed the trestle near Hampton's Station and also destroyed a water station. Within days, Union forces had quickly repaired the crossing.

The Union military continued to use the line until April 1865.

Toward the end of the war, thousands of ex-slaves gathered in the area after their liberation. Many joined the Union army, while hundreds lived in a shantytown along the river. As the Civil War wound down after the surrender of the Army of Northern Virginia at Appomattox Court House on April 9, 1865, a new normal grabbed hold of the MC&L and railroads across the former Confederacy. The railroad was in remarkably poor shape following years of fighting.

It must have been quite a scene to see trains operating over badly damaged track and crumbling infrastructure. The wood used on bridges up and down the line was rotten, switches didn't function and the bridge over the Cumberland River—an accomplishment that brought the railroad such pride just a few years earlier—was inoperable. In 1865, for the railroad,

Famed photographer George N. Barnard took this picture of a fortified railroad bridge across the Cumberland River in Nashville during the Civil War. An 1858 newspaper account indicates that the bridge in Clarksville would look similar to the Nashville structure. *Library of Congress.*

beginning in the woods and ending in a hollow tree was a pipe dream—it more or less existed only in theory.

By July 1865, citizens were eagerly awaiting the formal reopening of the line. "There is much work to be done upon it," the *Clarksville Chronicle* reported, noting that important bridges, such as the one across the Tennessee River, lay in ruins. The local newspaper appealed to the residents of Louisville to help with restoring the line to its antebellum glory:

> *We think our sister city of Louisville should have an eye toward seeing this road put again in working order. She has done much for it—acted with a liberality truly noble, and characteristic of her people. Our own city can do*

but little towards raising the funds necessary to complete the work. Money is scarce, trade is depressed and the capital in the hands of people is too small to effect much. All that she can do though, will be freely done. But are there not other parties interested in putting this project through? The country through which it passes is rich in undeveloped resources, and may be regarded as a field almost unsurpassed in interest to the agriculturist and capitalist. We hope that before the close of the coming fall, trade and travel may be resumed on this line between Louisville and Memphis, and that the prospect, once so bright for its success as a main thoroughfare connecting the Mississippi with the Ohio, may yet be realized.[203]

The newspaper reported that restoring the line would cost an estimated $210,000 plus an additional $200,000 for rolling stock. Meanwhile, even as various parties connected to the railroad sought to confirm next steps, the second mortgage bond holders filed suit in Montgomery County Chancery Court "to foreclose a mortgage made by the company for the payment of said bonds....Should the complainants obtain a decree for the sale of the road, it will necessarily delay active operations upon its repairs for some time."

By August 1865, the *Nashville Daily Union* reported that "travel on the Memphis Branch of the Louisville and Nashville railroad from Bowling Green to Clarksville is remarkably good, and unless indications are deceptive, it is a paying institution." The article also noted:

Upon the evacuation of this portion of the country by the rebels after the fall of Fort Donelson, they burned one span of the railroad bridge where it crosses the Cumberland river at Clarksville. Since then, and until the rebellion was crushed out, a good portion of the country west of the river between Clarksville and Memphis has been infested with guerilla bands and frequent raids made into it by detachments of the rebel army. The Government considering, we suppose, that no practical utility could result in an effort to reconstruct and keep open the road, never took any steps in that direction; consequently the road has been a dead letter, with the exception of that portion referred to above, since the rebellion broke out. I understand it is the purpose of the Company to put the [road] in running order through to Memphis at an early day.[204]

By September 1865, the railroad bridge across the Red River was out of service. "It is exceedingly inconvenient to passengers to have to halt at the Fair Grounds," the *Clarksville Weekly Chronicle* declared, calling on the railroad to repair the crossing.[205] The bridge was presumably repaired by

Nashville, Tennessee, pictured here in 1864, was an important logistics hub during the Civil War. The Tennessee state capitol is visible in the background. *Library of Congress.*

late November 1865, when the railroad announced it planned to start an accommodation between Clarksville and the Tennessee-Kentucky state line for "comers and goers." The train was scheduled to leave the state line in the morning and return in the evening.[206]

Somehow, in the midst of this chaos, the railroad returned to service during the waning years of the Civil War, but profits remained elusive.[207]

The Civil War left its mark on Middle Tennessee just as it did the entire country. In order to operate again, the MC&L would need to be rebuilt from the ground up, a process that would take the better part of a year. But time was the easy part of the rebuild—it would also require a significant amount of resources to return the railroad to running order. The problem was that the Memphis, Clarksville & Louisville didn't have the resources needed to undertake such a task, which ultimately spelled disaster for the line.

TABLE 1

According to the 1864–65 Louisville & Nashville annual report, the Memphis, Clarksville & Louisville reported the following earnings and expenditures for its fourteen-mile line between the Tennessee–Kentucky state line and Clarksville. [Note: The numbers have been reproduced from the original source but do not tally.]

Date	Expenditures	Earnings
July 1864	$977.48	$938.32
August 1864	$918.77	$802.91
September 1864	$2,142.36	$812.61
October 1864	$1,596.38	$732.82
November 1864	$1,006.04	$849.55
December 1864	$1,112.42	$649.51
January 1865	$1,215.52	$822.20
February 1865	$1,059.57	$764.90
March 1865	$1,220.20	$1,112.32
April 1865	$1,113.93	$1,269.25
May 1865	$1,321.22	$963.33
June 1865	$2,727.29	$1,940.54
Adams Express, 12 months	-	$960.52
TOTAL	$16,411.18	$12,628.78

POSTWAR REBIRTH

Following the war, communities across the ravaged southern United States turned attention to rebuilding, including infrastructure. When the Civil War ended, the South found its railroads—and roads in general—to be in a state of disarray. The Memphis, Clarksville & Louisville was no different.

On June 24, 1865, the MC&L asked Tennessee governor William G. Brownlow to appoint a receiver—specifically, George T. Lewis, who moved to Clarksville when he was sixteen years old, just prior to the start of the Civil War—to oversee operations and repairs. Brownlow obliged, and in July 1865, he appointed Lewis, a native of Delaware County, Pennsylvania, to the post. For his service, Lewis received a salary of $5,000 per year.[208] The task before him was monumental. Repairing the railroad required significant capital the company did not have.

In addition to the physical upgrades required for the line, the railroad had no rolling stock at the time Lewis took charge. He remedied this by purchasing a dozen locomotives and a number of freight cars from the federal government. "This rolling stock was not the very best, as it had been culled over before Mr. Lewis made his purchase," G.B. Faxon, a railroad official, later testified.[209] Lewis also built a new passenger depot in Clarksville.

In the wake of the Civil War, the community had a long list of infrastructure needs. Accordingly, the July 14, 1865 edition of the *Clarksville Weekly Chronicle* argued there was "no one thing demanding immediate attention more than

William G. Brownlow (1805–1877) was the seventeenth governor of Tennessee and served from April 5, 1865, until February 25, 1869. *Library of Congress.*

the Red River Bridge on the Russellville Turnpike," apparently prioritizing the restoration of a turnpike ahead of the railroad.

On August 8, 1865, Secretary of War Edwin M. Stanton ordered the U.S. Army to formally relinquish control of Tennessee railroads and return them to their owners:

> *Each company will be required to give bonds satisfactory to the government that they will, in twelve months from the date of transfer as aforesaid, or such other reasonable time as may be agreed upon, pay a fair valuation for the government property turned over to said companies, the same being first appraised by competent and disinterested parties at a fair valuation, the*

United States reserving all government dues for carrying mails, and other service performed by each company until said obligations are paid; and if at the maturity of said debt the amount of government dues retained as aforesaid does not liquidate, the same the balance is to be paid by the company in money.

About six weeks after Stanton's order, on September 23, 1865, the government returned the line to the railroad company.[210]

On October 13, 1865, the *Clarksville Weekly Chronicle* noted that repairing the MC&L "demands the earnest and immediate attention of all concerned." It added that "the entire line hence to Memphis remains as it is, it is worse than useless, because the interest has to be paid upon the capital; and unless it is to be speedily put in running order, by the present company, it had better be sold to parties who have the means to make it available to trade, and a benefit to the country through which it passes."

The railroad bridge over the Tennessee River in Bridgeport, Alabama, was destroyed during the Civil War. Here, a pontoon bridge is under construction next to the railroad bridge. This scene repeated itself across the Confederacy, including on the MC&L's Tennessee River crossing. *Library of Congress*.

The following day, Stanton issued an order authorizing Thomas to sell rolling stock "not needed by the United States for actual use" to southern railroads. The order required railroads to repay the federal government "the full appraised value of the property sold to them, in equal monthly installments" plus interest. Railroads did receive credit for any military transport.

In November, receiver George T. Lewis appointed George B. Fleece, who was an official with the MC&L before the war, as superintendent and engineer and George B. Faxon as treasurer.[211] "We have no doubt that these appointments will meet the approbation of all concerned," the *Clarksville Chronicle* trumpeted. Fleece "knows all about the road, and is, therefore, the fittest person to take it in hand." Faxon, meanwhile, "has had much experience in the business which he is called upon to discharge, and has given entire satisfaction. His appointment is gratifying to his friends, and can not fail to be acceptable to the parties more immediately interested."[212]

There was no shortage of repairs for the new leadership team to tackle. According to a December 1865 newspaper report, the depot was returned to order for receiving freight, and trains were running twice a day to and from Tait's Station. Walter Neblett was appointed freight agent in Clarksville "and is now ready to receive and ship by railroad produce and freight of every description," the *Clarksville Weekly Chronicle* reported.[213]

Meanwhile, Fleece declined the appointment of superintendent, and the position was subsequently offered to G.C. Breed, "who proved his competency for the position by his agency in the original construction of the road."[214]

Passenger trains heading to the state line left Clarksville at 6:00 a.m., and the returning train arrived at 8:35 a.m. The evening train left Clarksville at 3:30 p.m., and the returning train arrived at 6:10 p.m.[215]

In January 1866, the Tennessee legislature approved a $400,000 loan for the railroad. "This furnishes the means of putting the entire road under contract in a very short time," the *Clarksville Weekly Chronicle* reported in its January 23, 1866 edition.

In February 1866, railroad officials began repairing the road, approving contracts with Bristol & Co. to rebuild trestles across the Tennessee and Cumberland Rivers and fix "defective trestle work" between Clarksville and Paris.[216] By February, "several shipments of men and material have been made to Cumberland City and Palmyra for the M. C. & L. R.R.," the *Clarksville Weekly Chronicle* reported. "This looks like work in earnest."[217]

On February 9, 1866, the *Clarksville Weekly Chronicle* estimated that the railroad, with the exception of the bridge across the Tennessee River,

Fighting during the Civil War wreaked havoc on railroads. Here, workers near Murfreesboro, Tennessee, repair a section of track after the Battle of Stones River in 1863—this was a common scene across the South in the wake of fighting. *Library of Congress.*

would be back in action by April 1, 1866.[218] The Tennessee River bridge, the newspaper projected, would be finished by July 1, 1866. As usual, the newspapers were overly optimistic. Apparently taking a cue from antebellum optimism, newspaper reports seemed to be a bit out of touch with the railroad's financial situation, which remained dire. In a March 10, 1866 letter, receiver George T. Lewis said the railroad was "not able to meet interest promptly upon bonds granted to said company."[219]

Lewis also stated that "during the first year of the war the bridges upon the road were all destroyed, excepting one permanent and one draw-bridge over the Cumberland river; also the greater portion of the [trestle] on the line of the road, and the road-bed itself has been greatly injured during the past five years—cuts filling up and embankments being washed away."

That meant the railroad had major repairs to make before it could resume service and try to refill its coffers. Rebuilding the line required laborers, but the railroad had difficulty hiring help and paid higher rates just to secure the necessary manpower. While the railroad worked to restore service, Lewis noted:

> *All of the means appropriated by the Legislature will be required for the rebuilding of bridges, and repairs necessary to put the road in good condition; consequently, I shall not have any means to meet the monthly instalments due the United States government, the collection of which has up to this time been suspended by Major General Thomas, commanding* [220]

The L&N helped the cause when it loaned $150,000 to the MC&L to help repair the railroad. As collateral security for the repayment of the loan, the MC&L gave the L&N $220,000 in state bonds that lawmakers had approved in January 1866.

An agreement between the two companies required the MC&L to return its line, with the exception of the Tennessee River bridge, to running order in four months; the company had six months to repair the crossing over the Tennessee River. The contract also stipulated that if the MC&L did not have sufficient motive power or rolling stock to carry through trains, the L&N had the power to operate its own trains over the line "by making a fair compensation." It also prevented the MC&L from granting any "privileges or lower rates" to other railroads "not also granted to the" L&N.

A missing span in the bridge over the Cumberland River was to be replaced toward the end of March 1866. It would be ready for the "passage of trains" in a matter of days.[221] As Lewis pointed out:

> *But, in consequence of the embarrassed condition of the road, financially, I am satisfied the instalments due to the United States government cannot be met for some time to come, as the proceeds of the road will be required for the betterment of the road, so as to make it what it should be, a first class road.* [222]

Lewis asked the government "to suspend the collection of the claim of the United States government for two years," noting that most "have been greatly embarrassed by the prostration of their business for the past five years." After two years, Lewis predicted, "the monthly instalments will be met promptly." The government ultimately agreed. However, in a May

18, 1866 letter, U.S. Army colonel Alexander Bliss, who served as assistant quartermaster general of the Union forces during the Civil War, wrote:[223]

The Secretary of War has approved recommendation of Major General Thomas, respecting the extension of time of payment asked for by the Memphis. Clarksville and Louisville Railroad Company, of its indebtedness to the United States for the purchase of railway material and supplies. The extension of time of payment is granted upon the following terms:

The company shall execute a bond to the United States in the penal sum of six hundred and seventy-four thousand one hundred and sixty-four dollars and twenty-two cents, ($674,164 22,) being double the amount of purchase, conditional for the payment in two years from the date of purchase, (November 30, 1865,) of one instalment of one twenty-fourth part of the purchase money, together with accrued interest at 7 3/10 per cent per annum, and the payment of the balance in twenty-three equal instalments, monthly, thereafter, with interest at the same rate per cent.

Further conditional, that if the receipts of the Memphis, Clarksville and Louisville railroad will justify it, the payments of instalments shall commence at an earlier date than November 30, 1867.

Respectfully, your obedient servant,
ALEXANDER BLISS,
Colonel, Q.M. Department, in charge Fourth division.
Captain S. R. Hamill,
Assistant Quartermaster, Nashville, Tennessee.

The MC&L faulted on its Tennessee Bonds in July 1866.

Even as railroad leaders tried their best to secure financial relief and return the road to running order, tragedy struck in May 1866, when a western span of the Cumberland River bridge collapsed, sending a construction train with sixteen or eighteen men on board into the Cumberland River. One man was killed in the fall. "If we have…been correctly informed, nearly all on the train fell into the river, and hence it is the more astonishing, how, after the tremendous shock of the fall, so many managed to swim to the shore," the *Clarksville Weekly Chronicle* reported.

A newspaper account indicates rotten timber that appeared to be sound may have led to the tragedy, prompting the publication to issue a call to railroad managers to "keep a constant inspection of all wooden structures on their roads….If they fail to heed the lesson this accident has taught them, they will be little less than guilty of murder for any future loss of life that may result from a like cause."[224]

The tragedy certainly put the spotlight on infrastructure up and down the MC&L line—a theme that would remain front and center in the coming years. The "falling of the permanent span of the bridge on the Cumberland river…necessitates the rebuilding of that and the draw-span…and inasmuch as many of the trestles on the line of road have been, and are being repaired, and as the falling of the span of bridge on the Cumberland—not being seven years old; casts a suspicion on the wood work of the entire line, it is proper, indeed it is demanded, that several of the trestles already repaired be entirely renewed," wrote receiver George T. Lewis in a May 21, 1866 letter to Tennessee governor William G. Brownlow.[225]

Finding it necessary to soldier on, Gilbert C. Breed, back in the role of superintendent and chief engineer, traveled to Cincinnati in May 1866 to procure a new bridge to replace the Cumberland River span that had collapsed earlier in the month. Breed asked the *Louisville Daily Courier* to report that "he does not believe that the accident…was caused by any defect in the plan of the McCallum bridge, or any fault in its construction; but that the accident was occasioned by the interior rotting of the timbers, which were, perhaps, put up too green, but which defects could not be discovered from outside observation."[226] While rotten timbers are certainly a plausible explanation for the collapse, Breed had an incentive to absolve contractors of any wrongdoing, as his company was involved in the construction of the bridge.

In May 1866, the railroad's directors elected George T. Lewis as president and George B. Faxon as treasurer, positions the two held for some months, even if in an unofficial capacity. "Mr. Lewis has displayed untiring energy in pressing forward the repairs of the road, and his past, is ample security for his future devotion to the duties of his office."[227] For his services, the railroad paid Lewis $5,000 per year.[228]

Seemingly unfazed, Lewis was optimistic about the railroad's ability to rebuild and ultimately turn a profit so it would not be a burden on the state. "I beg, sir, to say that the prospects of a lucrative business—a profitable business over the railroad is very flattering, and I feel satisfied the State will in the end lose nothing by her liberality and kindness to this road," Lewis wrote in his May 21, 1866 letter to Governor Brownlow.[229]

In a September 12, 1866 report sent to Brownlow, Lewis detailed the monumental task facing the railroad. Engineers who examined the line "stated that no part of the road was in condition to pass trains safely, except for that portion lying east of Clarksville, thirteen miles in length," Lewis noted.[230] The railroad to the west of Clarksville—effectively between the city and Paris—required "extensive repairs." Nearly the entirety of the seventy-mile stretch "was covered with weeds, briers and bushes." Cuts along the route were filled, embankments were destroyed and bridges needed to be rebuilt. It "was impossible to use a locomotive on any part of the road," Lewis wrote.

While the repairs that would be necessary to return the road to running order were major, the situation was compounded by the fact the railroad found it difficult to recruit help. Lewis noted in his report:

> *In the first place it was impossible to draw labor from roads in operation to this one, without increasing the pay as an inducement. Consequently, I was compelled to pay day laborers, foremen and mechanics about twenty-five per cent, above usual rates.*[231]

Despite this, Lewis was optimistic about the future of the railroad, writing, "I am pleased to state, sir, that the prospect for business is decidedly good"—and the numbers seemingly supported his claim.[232]

Service Resumes

Postwar service resumed on the Memphis, Clarksville & Louisville on August 13, 1866. The railroad, along with the Memphis & Ohio and the Louisville & Nashville, reached an operational accord, "arrangements having been made by the three companies to operate their roads as one line, under the name of the Memphis & Louisville Railroad."[233] The excitement leading up to the resumption of service was palpable, and the editor of the *Paris Intelligencer* planned to host a massive picnic as soon as train service resumed.[234]

Two passenger trains were scheduled to run daily between Louisville and Memphis.[235] However, their precise timing was initially unclear. "But whatever may be the bitterness of the past, or the uncertainly of our political future, the restoration of this great artery of social and commercial life, is an episode that should be hailed with delight, and that should receive some fitting celebration at the hands of the communities, whom it has re-united," the *Clarksville Weekly Chronicle* noted on August 10, 1866.

During the first eighteen days of its return to operation, between August 13 and August 31, the railroad averaged more than $400 per day in business. "I feel confident, sir, that the income of this road will, ere long, be sufficient to pay current expenses, make necessary improvements along the line, and meet the interest due to the State," Lewis said in the conclusion of a September 12, 1866 report.[236]

To bring the road into working condition, Lewis's report indicated that the railroad spent a total of $49,350, including:

$7,000 on boiler and lathes

$20,000 on railroad iron and spikes

$2,000 on seats for three passenger coaches

$1,200 on stationery, blanks, books and tickets

$1,000 for fees on state bonds

$1,150 for repairs on an engine bought from the U.S. government

$4,000 to cover the machine shop with iron

$2,500 on the railroad's eating house and offices, which were unfinished at the time

$3,000 for hand trucks and cars[237]

Understanding the value of its Memphis Branch, shortly after the Civil War, the L&N offered to purchase the road, hoping to create a single railroad between Louisville and Memphis. MC&L officials, "having no means to put the road in order," did not accept the offer. The L&N even offered to operate the line "and to apply the net earnings to the redemption of the debt. Unfortunately this proposition was not accepted, and a whole year's business was thus lost."[238] In an 1866 report, the L&N noted:

> Arrangements have been made with the two connecting lines for the operation of the road to Memphis, in effect the same as if it was under the control of one company. Passengers will not have to change cars between Louisville and Memphis, and freight will go through without break of bulk. One day and two nights is all the time required to put freight from Louisville to Memphis, and vice versa. This arrangement, it is hoped, will, when fully known among business men, induce a large amount of freight to go over this line.

In its December 7, 1867 edition, the *American Railroad Journal* aptly summed up the situation, saying the MC&L's "managers…guided somewhat by

44   THE LOUISVILLE AND

LOCAL PASSENGER TARIFF.

MEMPHIS BRANCH.

No's	Name of Stations.	Fare.
81	Clarksville to Louisville.	$7 35
80	Cherry's " "	7 10
79	Hampton's "	7 00
78	Tait's " "	6 90
77	State Line " "	6 75
76	Hadensville "	6 65
75	Allinsville "	6 45
74	Olmstead "	6 30
73	Whippoorwill "	6 20
72	Russellville "	5 85
70	McLeod "	5 60
69	Auburn "	5 40
68	South Union "	5 25
67	Rockfield "	5 10
32	Memphis Junction to Louisville	4 85
31	Bowling Green " "	4 70
30	Bristow " "	4 50
29	Oakland " "	4 20
28	Smith's Grove " "	4 10
27	Rocky Hill " "	3 95
26	Glasgow Junction " "	3 70
25	Cave City " "	3 50
24	Woodland " "	3 45
23	Horse Cave " "	3 30
22	Rowlett's " "	3 10
21	Munfordville " "	3 00
20	Bacon Creek " "	2 75
19	Upton " "	2 40
18	Sonora " "	2 25
17	Nolin " "	2 15
16	Glendale " "	2 05
15	Elizabethtown " "	1 75
14	Colesburg " "	1 40
13	Booth's " "	1 35
12	Lebanon Junction " "	1 25
11	Belmont " "	1 05
10	Bardst'n Junction " "	95
8	Shep. and Car. " "	75
7	Gap in Knob " "	65
6	Anderson's " "	60
5	Brook's " "	55
4	Deposit " "	35
3	Randolph's " "	30
2	Strawberry " "	25
1	Louisville.	....

Local passenger rates for the Memphis Branch were published in the 1867 *Travelers Guide to the Louisville Rail Road*. A trip from Clarksville to Louisville cost $7.35 (approximately $125 in 2019 dollars). *HathiTrust*.

popular prejudices and the desire to operate their road as an independent line, rejected this proposition, and accepted instead the bonds of the state, permitting the road to pass into the hands of a receiver."

In early August 1866, MC&L superintendent A.F. Goodhue and superintendents of other railroads across the state, including the Illinois Central and the Memphis & Ohio, met at the Gayoso House hotel, a longtime Memphis landmark built in the 1840s and noted for its modern luxury as envisioned by Robertson Topp, a former Memphis & Ohio official. There, they discussed aligning timetables to better allow passengers to make connections.[239] An updated timetable from the MC&L's newly appointed assistant superintendent Robert Meek appeared in the *Clarksville Chronicle* in October 1866. The condensed timecard listed arrivals and departures:

Leaves Louisville at 5:00 p.m. and 6:15 a.m.
Arrives at Louisville at 11:15 p.m. and 2:00 p.m.
Leaves Memphis at 11:00 p.m. and 4:00 p.m.
Arrives at Memphis at 2:45 a.m. and 9:00 a.m.
Leaves Nashville at 10:00 p.m. and 1:30 p.m.
Arrives at Nashville at 4:30 p.m. and 9:30 a.m.
Leaves Clarksville at 5:55 p.m. and 2:05 a.m.
Arrives at Clarksville at 12:25 p.m. and 5:00 p.m.

Restoration of the railroad also represented a reconnection to the outside world. In addition to bringing passengers, freight and mail, trains carried newspapers from other communities, giving residents a window onto the world around them.

Shortly after service resumed, the *Clarksville Weekly Chronicle* stated: "They were most delightful reminders of old times, and if the Memphis press will be happy to see something from Clarksville, as we were to greet their issues again, they will put us on their daily exchange list."[240]

In October 1866, receiver George T. Lewis invited the *Clarksville Chronicle* to join an excursion to Paris. The condition of the railroad had a profound impact on the newspaper. "During the trip we were especially struck with the splendid condition of the entire track on the route," said the newspaper report. "When we reflected upon the many and most discouraging disadvantages under which has been conducted, too much praise cannot be bestowed upon Mr. G.T. Lewis, the accomplished Receiver of the road, for the energy, fact and admirable management he has displayed in bringing the

The Gayoso House Hotel in Memphis, built in 1842, overlooked the Mississippi River. The prominent landmark, pictured here around 1887, burned down in 1899. *Wikimedia Commons.*

part of the road under his supervision, to is present high state of perfection. He is the right man in the right place."

The following month, the railroad announced it would receive sealed bids to lease the new eating house at the new railroad depot in Clarksville. The house included a dining room measuring 100 feet by 24 feet, four family rooms measuring 20 feet by 20 feet, a kitchen measuring 20 feet by 15 feet, a store room measuring 20 feet by 8 feet and a china closet measuring 20 feet by 8 feet. "The lessee will be required to furnish the establishment in a good style, and to keep a first-class Eating House." Based on train schedules at the time, passengers would take three meals per day at the eating house.[241]

By all accounts, the railroad attempted to up the ante on the service it offered. One such story, though vague, appeared in the November 30, 1866 edition of the *Clarksville Weekly Chronicle.* On some unknown date, a group of fifteen to twenty passengers was waiting for the train to take them to the connection with the Edgefield. Since the passenger train was running hours behind schedule, superintendent Robert Meek "had an extra train fitted up" so the group could make their connection. "Such courtesies are not unusual," gushed the newspaper.[242]

While it looked like some semblance of normalcy had returned to the railroad, not everyone was optimistic, and some members of the Clarksville community expressed a lack of optimism about the state of the MC&L. A December 1866 letter signed by "T." sought to refute the obvious consternation some members of the Clarksville community held toward the railroad:

It is a matter of some surprise and regret to me to hear persons in our own community, who are interested in the prosperity of our town, speak in disparaging terms of our road—surprised, because men who should be conversant with the history of our road "wonder" why there has not been a million dollars worth of work done with three or four hundred thousand dollars. It is, indeed, surprising to hear men, whose judgment we were wont to respect, speculating as to why our road is not in as good condition as any other road—why it is not ballasted, why old structures (altho reliable) have not been pulled down replaced by new, and why we have not new engines and rolling stock of every description. Indeed it would take two million dollars to do the work they are "wondering has not been done with five hundred thousand dollars in State bonds, which had to be sold at a heavy discount. In speaking thus, men not only do the road and our worthy Receiver an injury, but they thoughtlessly strike a blow at the interest of our town and their own pockets.

Now we claim for the road that in the single matter of finances, the Receiver, Mr. Lewis, has accomplished that which few would have undertaken, and saved to the State, by his superior financiering skill, between twenty and thirty thousand dollars; and for the most part has directed the repairs with an energy and skill commendable in one of so short experience in railroad matters. We further claim that at present the road is operated with great care and safety and that since its opening last August there has been but one accident of a serious character. The recent slide in Tennessee Ridge cut was unavoidably the effect of recent heavy rains. We believe that in everything, Mr. Lewis has had at heart the interest of the road, and under the circumstances has done the best he could, and therefore hope our citizens will render him the credit he so justly deserves, and cease to expect him to build a first class road without money.

In conclusion, we would like to notice the different officers on the road, but have only time to speak, briefly, of Mr. Robert Meek, Assistant Superintendent. Mr. Meek is one of those few Northern men whom we are willing to have amongst us, and besides being a gentleman of indomitable energy, is an old and experienced railroad Superintendent.[243]

Whatever independence the Memphis & Ohio and the MC&L had before the Civil War started to fade following the conflict, at least when it came to passenger through train operations.

A New Partnership

During the 1866–67 fiscal year, the Louisville & Nashville partnered with the Memphis, Clarksville & Louisville and the Memphis & Ohio "for a through business with those roads from Louisville to Memphis, hoping they would be able to put those roads in good order, and that the joint operation would be profitable to all parties. [The Memphis, Clarksville & Louisville has] not had the means to put the roads in condition."[244]

In a January 1, 1867 report, Jonathan R. Tapscott, assistant engineer, highlighted the amount of work completed on the line, including major repairs to the line's bridges. Among its work, the railroad rebuilt 769 linear feet of bridges and 4,064 linear feet of trestle on the railroad's western division, placed 35,000 ties in tracks on the railroad's western division and contracted for 50,000 ties on the railroad's eastern division[245]

An 1867 passenger guide said the journey over three different roads "will, for purposes of travel, operate as one, and passengers taking cars at Louisville may go through to Memphis without change."[246] Furthering the idea of a single, 377-mile-long operating entity, the railroads began operating under the name Louisville & Memphis (or Memphis & Louisville) Railroad. Work on the railroad and its facilities continued as the calendar flipped to 1867.

Interestingly, a timetable from MC&L superintendent Robert Meek in the October 16, 1867 edition of the *Weekly Patriot* indicated two northbound trains and two southbound trains every day. Northbound trains departed Clarksville at 4:00 a.m. and 2:00 p.m., while southbound trains left the city at 8:48 a.m. and 11:37 p.m. The timetable indicated connections at State Line with the Edgefield & Kentucky and the L&N.

The partnership was not an immediate success, however. The L&N advanced $123,775.11 to the MC&L and the Memphis & Ohio "without any immediate prospect of reimbursement." L&N officials "then thought of consolidating the roads by obtaining part of their stock and giving them part of ours, and providing for the debts of the roads and the means of putting them in good order for the joint benefit."[247]

Going Off the Rails

On December 7, 1866, a Memphis-bound train derailed a few hundred yards north of the trestle over Budds Creek, located roughly a dozen miles southwest of Clarksville and near Palmyra. As "the train was proceeding at the usual rate the tender attached to the engine suddenly jumped from the track. The coupling broke and the entire train, with the exception of the sleeping car, was precipitated into a deep mountain gully, down which was rushing a torrent of water. The cars were smashed almost to splinters, and the shrieks of the wounded are represented as having been terrible to listen to."[248]

The train's locomotive crashed "through the trestle work followed by the baggage car, the passenger coach and the sleeping car." Two people—James McGuire, the express agent, and an unidentified passenger from Germany—were killed. An additional twenty-five to thirty passengers were hurt in the crash, including the baggage master, Mr. Howard, who suffered a fractured leg and arm.[249]

Following the crash, injured passengers were transported to Clarksville; McGuire's body was transported to Nashville, where a funeral was held on December 9. "A large number of friends and acquaintances followed him to the grave," said a newspaper account. The St. Vincent de Paul Society and the Catholic Orphan Association took part in the ceremony. McGuire was buried in the Catholic Cemetery. The railroad repaired the roughly one hundred feet of trestle damaged in the derailment, and two days later, trains were again operating over the section of track.

By 1867, both the Memphis & Ohio and the MC&L were on the verge of bankruptcy. Infrastructure woes along the MC&L continued as the Tennessee River bridge was washed out, eliminating through service to Memphis from March 11 until April 13, 1867.[250] In its 1866–67 annual report, the L&N noted the operational problems with the Louisville-to-Memphis line:

> *Owing to the incomplete condition of the road south of State Line, the very unfavorable weather during the past winter, and the causes already mentioned above, besides the great difficulty which must always be experienced in managing satisfactorily a through line composed of several independent links, the results of the operation of the Memphis & Louisville Line have not been as favorable as was anticipated.*
>
> *The roads south of State Line are, however, now in a better condition, and it may reasonably be expected that during the coming year, under more favorable circumstances, the merits of this line will be more fully developed.*

Spotty service over the line wasn't the only issue, and the railroad's leadership was hardly any more steady. On March 5, 1867, the Tennessee House and Senate adopted a joint resolution instructing the governor to remove "the present Receiver" and "appoint another in his place." Shortly thereafter, George T. Lewis was removed as receiver (by the end of March 1867), and Captain S.B. Brown appointed as his successor on April 1, 1867.[251] While Lewis made $5,000 per year, Brown received an annual salary of $10,000—a rate Brown later testified was approved by Brownlow. The *Memphis Daily Appeal* noted:

> *The removal of Mr. G. T. Lewis from the office of Rail Road Receiver, created little surprise here, but rather added to popular contempt for the Legislature. Mr. Lewis, in his management of the road, displayed great skill, energy and integrity, and while we condole with the Company on the loss of such an officer, we heartily congratulate Mr. Lewis upon being freed from all connection with the foul crowd that removed him. Their opinion seems to be that, if the road can be brought under the exclusive control of yankees, the magic influence of the word, loyalty, will pay its debts and repair its damages. At any rate, the yankees will get the salaries and perquisites—a vital consideration with Radicals.[252]*

Restoring service on the Memphis & Louisville was certainly a boon to the L&N's business. Freight earnings over the entire Memphis & Louisville increased from $33,376.13 to $67,556.89 for the year ending on June 30, 1867.[253]

The railroad's finances and turnover in leadership had far-reaching consequences for the companies it employed. One such instance resulted in litigation against the railroad. Before his discharge, Lewis employed W.H. Bristol & Thomas Skidmore to build bridges along the line. When he was unable to pay them, he struck a new agreement with the company, which Brownlow approved:

> *Whereas I, George T. Lewis, receiver of the Memphis, Clarksville & Louisville Rail Road, appointed by the Governor of Tennessee, and acting for said state, employed W.H. Bristol and Thomas J. Skidmore, partners under the name and style of Bristol & Skidmore, to build certain bridges on the line of said Railroad, and now owe them for building the bridges over the Tennessee River, Jellico creek and a creek at Palmyra.*

The railroad owed Bristol and Skidmore $21,569.90 for their work. The contract outlined the following payment schedule:

$10,750.90 on December 7 next
$3,606.33 1/3, payable with interest from the first of November 1866,
on the first day of February 1867
$3,606.33 1/3, payable on with interest from the first day of November
1866 on the 1st of March 1867
$3,606.33 1/3 on April 1, 1867, payable with interest from the first day
of November 1866 on the first day of April 1867

Perhaps of most interest was another provision included in Lewis's agreement:

Therefore, in consideration of the promises and being anxious to secure the payment of said sum of money to said Bristol & Skidmore, I hereby pledge to them on behalf of the state of Tennessee, enough of the receipts, derived from the earnings of said rail road to fully pay off, and discharge all of the above named debts, and I hereby agree with said Bristol & Skidmore that all three of said bridges shall remain their property, as a pledge and security for the payment of said debts, with authority to remove them upon the failure of payments on the part of myself as receiver and agent of the state, this 1st day of November 1866.[254]

When the railroad could not pay the money it owed the company, the company sued the railroad and new receiver S.B. Brown. Brown, much like Lewis, "treated the claim of complainants with indifference," Bristol and Skidmore alleged.[255] Their suit further alleged "that the great public importance of this road have prevented them from aperting the extreme legal rights of complainants in taking [possession] of said bridges, and pulling them down and carrying them to other [locations], nor do they believe that they would be permitted to do so." Bristol and Skidmore asked the court to order Brown to bring into court information about the railroad's earnings and receipts and pay what the railroad promised for bridge construction. Bristol and Skidmore asked for the right to remove the bridges from the railroad line if necessary.

A chancellor in Clarksville decided that Bristol and Skidmore should execute a bond for $24,000, which would cover all costs and damages. The chancellor further ordered Brown to pay $2,000 per month to a third party who, in turn, would distribute the money to Bristol and Skidmore.

The railroad appealed the ruling, and it is unclear whether the court served the order on Brown. The case eventually made it to Tennessee's Supreme Court, which ruled it void.

A Louisville & Nashville Offer

The Montgomery County Court met on April 20, 1867, to weigh a Louisville & Nashville proposal to buy the Memphis, Clarksville & Louisville. A committee appointed by the L&N's board of directors proposed giving stockholders of the MC&L twenty-five cents on the dollar. Although action was initially deferred, on July 1, 1867, the court approved the proposal.[256]

However, the decision does not seem to have resulted in any action, likely because other jurisdictions and entities with a stake in the railroad's operations would have to agree. In fact, just a few days earlier, on June 22, 1867, G.A. Henry had been elected as the railroad's president, while George B. Faxon was named secretary and treasurer.[257]

Governor William Brownlow dismissed S.B. Brown as receiver on January 20, 1868, saying Brown never made a report about the railroad's account. "He has been called upon for his report, but has not yet submitted it," according to the *Nashville Union and Dispatch*. He "owes it to himself to make a speedy report to silence criticisms and suspicions of the public in regard to his management of that road."[258]

Brownlow appointed D.B. Cliffe as the railroad's new receiver. Cliffe earned an annual salary of $5,000 until July 14, 1868, and an annual salary of $3,000 until November 30, 1869, when his term ultimately ended.[259] On January 25, 1868, the railroad's directors, including G.A. Henry, Robert W. Humphreys, Joshua Cobb and Joshua Elder, sent a letter to Brownlow asking him, essentially, to pressure Cliffe to retain Robert Meek as the railroad's superintendent. Meek, a New York native who worked as a master mechanic and superintendent of the Indianapolis & Cincinnati Railroad, was initially appointed as assistant superintendent in October 1866 in the wake of superintendent A.F. Goodhue's departure.

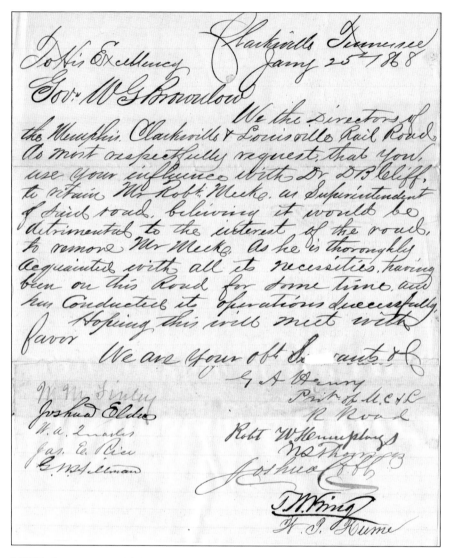

MC&L directors wrote this letter to Tennessee governor William G. Brownlow on January 25, 1868, asking the governor to use his influence with receiver D.B. Cliffe to retain Robert Meek as the railroad's superintendent. *University of Tennessee Special Collections.*

The directors wrote:

> *We the directors of the Memphis, Clarksville & Louisville Rail Road do most respectfully request that you use your influence with Dr DB [Cliffe], to retain Mr. Robt. Meeke [sic] as Superintendent of said road, believing it would be detrimental to the interest of the road, to remove Mr Meeke, as he is thoroughly acquainted with all its necessities, having been on this Road for some time, and has conducted its operations successfully.*[260]

Meek seemingly maintained his role with the railroad, but by February 1, 1868, employees went on strike "for the non-payment of wages due," according to a report in the *Detroit Free Press*.[261] The strike was short-lived and seemingly did not impact railroad operations, as news accounts indicate that at least some traffic moved over the line. While the action ended by February 4, 1868, it was a harbinger of a larger strike to come—one that would have a greater effect on the future course of the railroad.

Railroad employees delivered a handbill outlining their grievances and a proposed resolution. They proposed running no trains (except for mail trains) until they were paid. "Their case is a hard one, and where the fault lies we cannot tell," the *Clarksville Chronicle* concluded. Meanwhile, former receiver S.B. Brown promised to vindicate himself from any wrongdoing.[262]

It didn't much matter who said what. The die had been cast, and no amount of bickering or assigning blame would change the fact the railroad had no money. It had been in receivership since the war, and now it could not even pay its employees.

The railroad was clearly teetering on the brink of destruction. Days later, on February 6, 1868, MC&L trains stopped operating "due to an unwillingness on the part of its employees to work without being paid."[263] While this second, larger strike didn't signal the end of the railroad, it set into motion a series of events that ultimately did lead to its demise.

6

THE DEATH KNELL

W hen the money ran out on the Memphis, Clarksville & Louisville
Railroad, employees refused to work, and a nearly two-week strike
began on February 6, 1868. The strike came less than two years after postwar
train service formally returned to "normal" on August 13, 1866.

The return of regular service did not equate to immediate profits,
a fact the MC&L—much like the Memphis & Ohio to the west—soon
discovered. As such, both roads were on the verge of bankruptcy after
defaulting on state bonds. Salaries and bills went unpaid, eventually
leaving the railroads unable to operate. It came to a head on February
6, 1868, when trains on the MC&L stopped operating "due to an
unwillingness on the part of its employees to work without being paid,"
according to historian Kincaid Herr.[264]

For eleven days, the MC&L was dormant, and through trains bypassed the
railroad. The freight that normally operated over the MC&L now shipped
over the Nashville & McKenzie and Nashville & Northwestern railroads.
Grass began growing in the railroad's inactive tracks. Governor William G.
Brownlow vehemently opposed the strike. In a February 8, 1868 letter to
state legislators, he said:

I have received information to the effect, that, the employes [sic] *on the
Memphis, Clarksville & Louisville Railroad, are on a strike for back pay,
and have gone so far as to resolve as follows: "That, from and after this date,
until all the employes are paid, or satisfactorily guaranteed the payment of
all money due them, up to the time of D. B. Cliff's appointment as Receiver*

of the Road, no trains shall pass from the State line to Paris, except the Express car, to deliver the mail." This resolution has been formally signed by the Chairman and committee.

It is a little strange that no such strike was attempted under either of the former Receivers. The present Receiver, I regard as one of the best men in Middle Tennessee, and it is no fault of his that this lawless proceeding has been resorted to.

I regard the whole affair as a regular conspiracy against the State authorities and road. Without being able to identify the parties, I think it proper to lay the whole matter before the Legislature, that you may take such steps as you deem called for in such an emergency.

I do not propose to yield to the mob spirit of any combination, but I hope the Legislature will aid me in demonstrating to these men, that the State can do as well without the advantages of the road as the employes can without employment, or the citizens without the active operations of the road through its disloyal territory.

Certainly the Legislature will not allow such lawless measures to force the State into the payment of claims before they are audited and their justness and correctness, ascertained.

I propose, if the Legislature shall agree with me, to wind up the affairs of the road and sell it out, so as to secure the State's interests.

I must again remind the [General] Assembly of the importance of the enactment of more stringent laws in regard to our railroads generally, and particularly of those passing into the hands of Receivers.

The *Clarksville Chronicle* published the bulk of the statement in its February 21, 1868 edition. The newspaper, however, condemned the governor, whom it referred to as the "imp of darkness," for his remarks, calling them "a slander against men who are his superiors in everything that constitutes the christian [*sic*] and gentleman. But malice in him is as natural a secretion, as venom is in a serpent."[265]

The governor "professes to see in it a huge rebellion against the State and his imperial power and scruples not to charge said strike upon our citizens and the rebellious district through which the road runs," the paper said. "The charge is grossly false and as malicious as it [is] false.—Petty tyrants see rebellion in every manifestation of private or public virtue; it is the result of conscious guilt which makes cowards of the boldest."[266]

Dr. D.B. Cliffe, appointed the railroad's receiver on January 16, 1868, contended that he was not responsible for debts Captain S.B. Brown, the

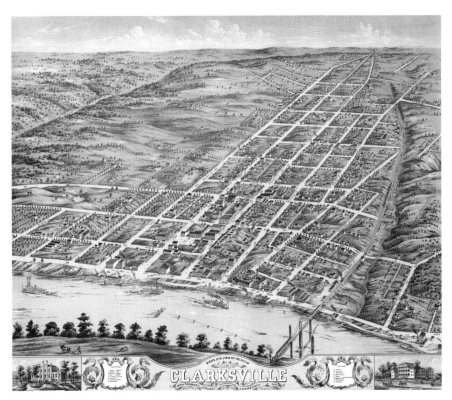

A bird's-eye view of the city of Clarksville as depicted in 1870. The railroad bridge across the Cumberland River is at lower right. *Library of Congress.*

railroad's former receiver, incurred. According to a February 8, 1868 article in the *Nashville Union and American*, the state's attorney general agreed. The *Nashville Union and American*, in its February 9, 1868 edition, perhaps best summarized the situation:

> *The Memphis, Clarksville and Louisville Railroad—Destitution of the Late Employes* [sic].—*Our readers have been informed, from time to time, of the embarrassments of the Memphis, Clarksville and Louisville railroad; how Receiver Brown was displaced and Dr. Cliffe substituted; how the employes* [sic] *failed to receive their pay, and were clamorous for it; and how a few days ago, the operations of the road were entirely suspended.*
>
> *This result has produced among the employes* [sic] *a condition of great destitution, which appeals to the public for charitable action. There were about two hundred of these* [employees] *on the road. Under the*

administration of Capt. Brown, they were not paid promptly their wages. Most of them, if not all, at the time of his removal, were due back pay from two to five months.

In the meantime they continued to work, and, of course, not having the money, run up board bills upon assurances that they would soon be paid off, and settle them up. When the road stopped, these anticipations were cut off, and boarding-house keepers and grocery merchants stopped their accounts by turning them off. They are now without means or credit, through no fault of their own, and in absolute want. They hope arrangements will soon be effected by the State authorities whereby the road will be again put in operation, and they be restored to employment.

But the day of calamity is upon them, and some of their generous friends desire their situation made public, that the benevolent may extend them some relief. Contributions for this purpose will be received by H. C. Sheetz, John Housley and Wm. Sippy, in this city and Edgefield. And any contributions left at this office will be promptly applied to their relief.

It is proper to say that Dr. Cliffe took charge of the road without funds— that he exerted himself to carry forward its operations—and that no blame is justly ascribable to him for the present condition of its affairs.[267]

Around this time, a group of eighty-five MC&L employees sent a request to the Tennessee General Assembly seeking the state's help in securing their pay:

We, the petitioners, would most respectfully petition your honorable body to devise some means whereby we may be enabled to get the money due us for service on the Memphis, Clarksville and Louisville Road, under the [administration] *of George T. Lewis and S. B. Brown, as receivers for the State. Some of us have been working said road ever since said road has been in the hands of the State, and from two to four months wages are now due us.*

Instead of selling the road to the larger L&N Railroad, MC&L officials sought to lease the company. They formally did so on February 20, 1868— an action that essentially extended the life of the railroad by about three years but did nothing to change its ultimate fate. James Guthrie, president of the L&N, and D.B. Cliffe, the MC&L's receiver, signed a contract for the L&N to "take charge of and run" the MC&L as an agent of the receiver and on behalf of the state. The agreement stipulated:

The Louisville and Nashville Railroad Company is to employ all the labor and purchase all the material necessary for the operation of the railroad, and make monthly payments [therefore] *out of the earnings of the road; and should the earnings exceed the operating expenses and necessary repairs, such excess is to be paid to said Receiver as the same accrues and is ascertained by proper settlements. The expenses for labor and material are to be first paid in full out of the earnings; and should the earnings not be sufficient for that purpose, the Louisville and Nashville Railroad Company is to pay such deficiency* [without charge to the State] *for said labor and material only, and is not to be responsible for any other matter or liability arising out of the operating of said railroad.*

The said railroad is to be operated in all respects as the property of the Memphis, Clarksville and Louisville Railroad Company, under the general advice and direction of said Receiver, but under the immediate control of the General Superintendent of the Louisville and Nashville Railroad Company as the agent of the Receiver, with power to appoint a local Superintendent with the advice of the Receiver. An exact account of all the earnings and expenditures in operating the road shall be kept by the Louisville and Nashville Railroad Company, and monthly reports and settlements shall be made between the parties. All payments to be made for labor and material as aforesaid by the Louisville and Nashville Railroad Company under this agreement, shall first be approved by the Receiver, before payment. The Louisville and Nashville Railroad Company is to have the right to collect all the earnings of the road, through the other agents of the Receiver employed as aforesaid by the Louisville and Nashville Railroad Company, and duplicate reports shall be made by said agents to the Receiver to enable him to keep correct accounts of the operations of the road. Necessary repairs are to be made out of the earnings; but no permanent improvements are to be made except with the joint consent of the parties, it being the purpose to operate the road in the most economical manner consistently with the safety and security of life and property.

Historian Maury Klein perhaps best summed up the situation, writing in his 1972 history of the Louisville & Nashville: "Some Memphis merchants continued to fear that L&N domination would result in commercial discrimination against their city....Goaded mainly by public clamor over this anxiety, the Clarksville rejected every L&N overture and vowed to operate the road free of outside control. While this stance met with popular approval, it led to financial disaster. The Clarksville lacked any resources to rehabilitate its line, and earnings failed to pay even operating expenses."[268]

In the end, the affair was rather unceremonious. On the third page of its February 21, 1868 edition, the *Clarksville Chronicle* noted: "We cannot say positively, but the impression is that this road has been leased to the Louisville and Nashville Railroad Company. At any rate, the hands are being paid off and the trains are running regularly." The next week, the newspaper reported, "The precise arrangement by which this road has been enabled to resume the running of its trains is variously stated."[269] If ever there were a single statement that summed up the railroad, it might be that one.

While the newspaper struggled to ascertain details, the L&N was in control of the MC&L. From February 17, 1868, to June 30, 1868, the railroad reported gross earnings of $79,422.47, including $42,308.85 from passenger and $31,114.99 from freight transportation. Express traffic was responsible for the balance—$2,998.63.[270] However, the railroad had operating expenses of $88,348.41. Coupled with expenses for materials on hand and advances made before the end of the 1868 strike, and the MC&L owed the L&N $26,139.23.[271]

In 2009, the State of Tennessee gave Montgomery County more than $900,000 to help rehabilitate the railroad bridge across the Cumberland River in Clarksville, pictured here in March 2002. *Railfanning.org.*

On May 30, 1868, the MC&L declared bankruptcy. On August 17, 1868, Edward H. East, an attorney for former receiver D.B. Cliffe, protested the bankruptcy filing, saying the company "could not take the benefit of the bankrupt law" passed in March 1867:[272]

The following proceedings before the Register in Bankruptcy, at Clarksville, a day or two since, will show the present status of this road:

For the Middle District of Tennessee.—David B. Cliffe, as Receiver of all the assets, franchises, rights and credits of the said railroad and its property by virtue of the laws of the State of Tennessee, files the following as objections to the application of the bankrupt laws to said road or its rights, franchises and assets:

1st. He denies the right of said railroad company to avail itself of the benefits of said act, and opposes and appeals from the adjudication heretofore made by the Register, allowing said railroad company to avail itself or themselves of said right.

2. He contests the right of the Register to appoint an assignee for said railroad company, and opposes the same.

3. He moves to dismiss the petition of said railroad company now filed with the Register in bankruptcy, asking to be allowed to take the benefit of said act of the Congress of the United States.

He opposes further prosecution of said matter in bankruptcy on other special or general reasons to be shown upon argument.

Edward H. East.
Sol. for Cliffe, Receiver.

In the District Court of the United States for the Middle District of Tennessee, in the matter of the Memphis, Clarksville and Louisville Railroad Company, in Bankruptcy at Clarksville in said district—I, J. Jay Buck, one of the Registers of said Court in Bankruptcy, do hereby certify, that in the course of the proceedings in said matter before me, the foregoing questions arose pertinent to the said proceedings, and were stated and agreed to by the counsel for the opposing parties, to wit: G.A. Henry and J.E. Bailey, who appeared for the State of Tennessee, one of the creditors of said bankrupt. Therefore, pursuant to section 4 of an act entitled "An act to establish a uniform system of bankruptcy throughout the United States," approved March 2, 1867, I hereby adjourn the same into court for decision by the Judge.

J. Jay Buck
Register in Bankruptcy.[273]

As legal matters progressed, the trains kept running. In May 1869, the 377-mile-long trip from Louisville to Memphis took approximately nineteen hours—an average speed of 19.8 miles per hour. MC&L locomotives burned a total of 8,450 cords of wood as its locomotives ran a total of 215,829 miles during the year ending June 30, 1869. L&N locomotives ran an additional 17,535 miles over the line.[274]

Table 2
According to the 1868–69 Louisville & Nashville annual report, Memphis, Clarksville & Louisville locomotive miles operated the following miles for the year ending June 30, 1869:

Locomotive Number	Passenger	Freight	Distributing	Total
1	643	927	11,897	13,467
2	1,340	14,334	2,617	18,291
3	13,209	8,585	925	22,719
4	9,694	837	3,674	14,205
5	3,688	1,355	10,718	15,761
6	-	13,250	3,069	16,319
7	-	30	960	990
8	7,502	13,362	460	21,324
9	6,846	17,769	176	24,791
10	17,882	3,640	270	21,792
11	18,531	5,287	952	24,770
12	19,839	1,384	177	21,400
TOTAL	99,174	80,760	35,895	215,829

In the midst of its legal woes, another tragedy struck the railroad in December 1868 when Conductor O'Brien, riding on top of the northbound freight train, "was knocked off by coming in contact with the bridge" near Erin, the *Clarksville Chronicle* reported in its December 11, 1868 edition. Several cars ran over him, killing him. "He was a courteous gentleman and a good conductor," the newspaper recalled.

While the railroad's leaders faced down a financial crisis and returned the railroad to some level of normalcy, they would soon face a greater catastrophe with far-reaching consequences.

Awful in the Extreme

E ugene Riley eased the No. 2 express train across the Montgomery County landscape. The train pulled out of the station at Paris at 9:40 p.m. Night had fallen, and the train was running on time. It was scheduled to steam for nearly twelve more hours, passing through Clarksville, Russellville and Bowling Green in the overnight hours before arriving in Louisville at 9:00 a.m., 190 track miles to the north.

The train began its journey at 3:00 p.m. on July 27, when it steamed out of Memphis. Speeds on the Louisville & Memphis were slow, but this particular route was an important one for passengers traveling between New York and New Orleans. In Humboldt, the Louisville-bound No. 2 express train added a "through" sleeping car from a New Orleans train.[275]

Up until that point, the trip was uneventful, and by 10:00 p.m., passengers had retired for the evening. The train—consisting of a locomotive, a baggage car owned by the L&N, a first-class car owned by the Memphis & Ohio, a second-class car owned by the L&N and a pair of sleeping cars owned by the Rip Van Winkle Sleeping Car Company—was due in Clarksville at 1:15 a.m.

By 1:00 a.m., the train was perhaps two minutes behind schedule as it approached the bridge over Budds Creek—a crossing consisting of "four spans of short wooden girder bridges joined to a trestle." Because the railroad rebuilt the line after the Civil War, the trestle was said to be just two years old, and the bridges three. Coincidentally, Budds Creek was the scene of a fatal crash less than three years earlier, but that thought likely did not enter anyone's mind in the early morning hours of July 28, 1869.

What happened next became the subject of considerable debate. According to some accounts, the train's speed increased. Two passengers from New Orleans—identified as Mr. Doll and Mr. White—allegedly arose, dressed and inquired as to what the problem might be. As the train approached the Budds Creek crossing, the engineer sounded the whistle, which was odd, considering there was no requirement for him to do so at this location.[276]

Moments later, the bridge gave way, and the train crashed into the creek bed below. Fire began to consume the train's cars. Only the sleeping car at the rear of the train did not fall into Budds Creek. Five people ultimately died as a result of the wreck.

"As described by those who were aboard the ill-fated train when it went down, the situation was awful in the extreme," stated a report in the *Federal Union* newspaper of Milledgeville, Georgia. The ensuing fire "made nearly a complete ruin of the train and its contents."[277]

A Deadly Chain of Events

The wreck at Budds Creek is arguably the most significant and calamitous event in the railroad's history and cast a pall over the company for the rest of its short existence. The disaster sparked headlines in newspapers across the nation, but from the first ink to hit the page, news accounts varied wildly in terms of the facts and circumstances surrounding the disaster. The crash happened at a time when the railroad was struggling financially and operationally and, ultimately, helped expedite its demise.

The *Federal Union* newspaper picked up one account of the wreck:

About one o'clock the sleeping travelers were awakened by a sudden rough movement of the train, as if it were off the track. After this jolting motion the train appeared to come to a stand still, and those who had been aroused congratulated themselves that all was right again. Just at that instant, they say, the train was on a poise ready to fall over the trestle height. In another second the whole line of cars had pitched downward and lay a crushed and ghastly heap in the basin of the creek. Notwithstanding the turning and shattering of the cars, and the indiscriminate wreck of human beings, hardly a voice was heard. The stillness was as profound as death.... The speed was so high that it carried the train under the track on the other side of the creek. The train fell in a zigzag or letter S position, and so lay upon the ground.

This report in the *Memphis Daily Appeal* on July 29, 1869, was one of the first accounts of the disaster at Budds Creek. *Library of Congress.*

The locomotive—L&N No. 17—was a standard steamer of the day, with four large sixty-six-inch driving wheels. New York's Schenectady Locomotive Works built the 54,000-pound locomotive, which had served on the L&N since July 1864. No. 17 was a workhorse of the railroad, running 18,347 miles in passenger service in the year ending June 30, 1869; this passenger service accounted for more than 99 percent of the locomotive's total service for the year.

As the train dragged on across the Middle Tennessee landscape, some passengers, like Sam P. Rose, tried to catch a wink of sleep. Rose was in a semiconscious state when the crash woke him. First, the locomotive toppled off the bridge and into the abyss, followed by the express and baggage cars, then a passenger coach. Some accounts make it seem as though the wreck happened in slow motion.

One passenger—identified only as an editor—aboard the train awoke to the sound of "the engine blowing on brakes" followed "by a rattling noise similar to that made by drawing a stick quickly across a picket fence."[278] Seconds later, the train crashed, throwing the writer "violently against a seat on the opposite side of the car." Splinters and shards of glass flew across the coach. "After extricating myself from the mass of rubbish as best I could, and ascertaining that I had received no serious injury, my next thought was to examine my surroundings, and decide upon a plan of action."[279]

The roof of the car in front of the sleeping car "was entirely gone, and nothing was between us and a cloudless sky." Passengers immediately jumped into action, pulling other passengers from the burning train and placing them in an area covered with weeds and briers, "which gave the scene an additional gloomy and desolate appearance. They had to be beaten down, and the roughness of the ground made it necessary to carry the sufferers sometimes to a considerable distance." Rescuers also had to clear passengers from the dangers of the burning train and pulled car seats, mattresses and pillows from the wreckage in a bid to make the injured as comfortable as possible.[280]

Amid the carnage and chaos at Budds Creek, stories of heroism emerged. Conductor Matt Lowe, a well-regarded railroad employee, calmly helped passengers move away from the wreckage. Frank W. Carney, a passenger (and son of former Montgomery County resident H.P. Carney), similarly jumped into action "with an almost superhuman effort" to aid fellow injured passengers.[281] An account in the *Daily Phoenix* newspaper (based in Columbia, South Carolina) relayed:

> *As soon as those who were but slightly disabled recovered from the shock, they set about extricating the less fortunate of their companions. The dead and maimed were all removed to the most comfortable localities around, and the cushions and bedding from the wrecked cars were happily brought into use. It is a fact not a little singular that the children, of whom there was a goodly number, were perfectly quiet during the desperate accident, and without exception escaped uninjured.*
>
> *While the unhurt passengers were humanely engaged in releasing and caring for those incapable of helping themselves, the debris of the train took fire from the engine furnace. This occurrence, dire as it might have appeared, created no undue excitement, owing to the precautions adopted by the cool-headed men performing the work of extrication. The fire burned slowly, beginning at the engine and gradually approaching the rear sleeping coach. The entire train and contents, as we have stated, were consumed, except the New Orleans sleeping car, which was badly damaged. Nearly all of the bridge and trestle-work also fell a prey to the conflagration.*

Sadly, not everyone could be saved. In the locomotive, steam escaping from the damaged boiler claimed the lives of engineer Riley and fireman Charles Shields. Riley, a Bowling Green resident, left behind a wife and a child. The engineer "was regarded as one of the most discreet engineers on the road he served and stood high in the estimation of all who knew him."[282] He "was scrupulously circumspect with his locomotive, always complying with the rules by which engine-drivers are governed, especially as to slow running over bridges and trestles."[283] Shields also lived in Bowling Green and similarly left behind a wife and children.

Table 3
This list of passengers involved in the wreck at Budds Creek was culled from various newspaper accounts and represents the best attempt to verify the correct spellings of names:

Fatalities	
Engineer Eugene Riley	Bowling Green
Fireman Charles Shields	Bowling Green
Hugh McColl	New Orleans
Susan McColl	New Orleans
Thomas Baxter (also identified as Thomas Shields and John Baxter)	Nashville or Carbondale, Mississippi
Injured Crew Members	
Brakeman Ed. Boone	
Baggage Master Charles A. Brown	
Express Messenger John C. Dugan	
Sleeping Car Conductor Sam Lewis	
Brakeman C.B. Webster	
Mail Agent W.W. (or W.D.) Wray	
Injured passengers	
J.J. Buck	Clarksville
John Burt (or Bart)	Columbia (or Columbus), Mississippi
Judge and Mrs. H.C. Caulkins and their two children	New Orleans
J. O'Donnell (Or J.L. Connell, J. O'Connell or J.S. Connell)	Stewart Station
C.H. Doge (or Sage)	Fulton, New York
Mr. and Mrs. Nolan Fontaine and their three children	Memphis
Lou (perhaps Louise) Gholson	Clarksville
J.C. Hannah	Coffeeville, Mississippi

Seth (or Sethe or Lethe) Henderson	Memphis
Captain Langdon	Mobile, Alabama
J.C. Levy	Holly Springs, Mississippi
William McCall	New Orleans
H.B. Michael	New Orleans
Hattie Michael (or Mitchell)	Lauderdale, Mississippi
Joseph Nutt (or Mut)	New Orleans
W.S. Packer (or Parker)	Pittsburg
Mr. and Mrs. Patterson	Baton Rouge, Louisiana
F.F. Porter	Paris
Barton Salisbury	Stewart Station
Mrs. Sawyer	
W.C. (or W.E.) Shephard (or Shepherd or Sheppard)	New Orleans
Ed. Stowe (or Stoull or Stone or Stover)	Eufaula, Alabama
Joseph West	
Walter Wilcox	Clarksville
Mr. Wood	New Orleans

Also among those killed was Hugh McColl, a native of Scotland who had moved to New Orleans twenty-five years earlier. The esteemed cotton merchant, along with his wife, Susan, and son, Norman, was traveling east "on a tour of pleasure." McColl was laying "in his berth" in a car at the rear of the train when it crashed. A piece of the coach's timber collapsed onto him, killing McColl and severely wounding his wife. Following the wreck, his body was transported to Cave Hill Cemetery in Louisville, while his wife was taken to St. Joseph's Infirmary. She died on August 2 from injuries sustained in the wreck.

Following the wreck, workers found the badly burned body of a man in the wreckage. At least one report identifies passenger Thomas Shields as another victim of the calamity, while another report identifies the victim as Thomas Baxter.[284] It seems likely that at least one of the stories incorrectly stated the fourth victim's last name, and some reports merely list the victim as a man named Baxter.

The wreck left at least twenty-five passengers and train personnel injured—some more severely than others. If nothing else, the hometowns of the wounded—which included Fulton, New York; Columbus, Mississippi; and Baton Rouge, Louisiana—illustrated how far and wide origins were for the passengers who rode over the MC&L. The No. 2 train, in particular, was a popular option for travelers between New Orleans and New York.

Charles A. Brown, the train's baggage master, was discovered buried under fallen timbers, baggage and freight, including several boxes of peaches. "Notwithstanding all this, he gave utterance to no moans or groans, was perfectly calm and collected, and quietly indicated to those who were assisting him, the portions of his body that were cramped by surrounding objects."[285] In all, he broke his right arm and suffered a small gash over his right eye. Passenger Edward Stone (or Stowe) of Eufaula, Alabama, suffered a broken thigh. Others, such as sleeping car conductor W.E. Wray and brakeman Edward Brown, escaped with relatively minor injuries.

The fire created an unexpected danger. Passengers fleeing the wreckage left behind their pistols. As the raging fire reached the guns, it discharged the ammunition inside the train.[286] Of the post-wreck scene, one passenger (who was not seriously injured) wrote:

> *The wails of the wounded smote the air behind and before us, and no time was to be lost in relieving the distress of those who were not able to help themselves. The more fortunate of the passengers did their duty in this regard nobly, and in all directions men with heads tied up with handkerchiefs and hands dripping with blood might be seen lifting from the wreck men and women whose cries and moans told too plainly of their sufferings. I do not think that there was on the train a man who was able to render service to the badly injured who did not yield it cheerfully.*[287]

Despite the level of injuries, some escaped unharmed. One passenger, identified as Miss Whittaker of New Orleans, was also in the train's rear sleeping car when the train plunged into Budds Creek. She escaped unharmed. Another passenger wrapped her child in "cushions, quilts and pillows." The child was pulled from the wreckage "as sound and lively as though nothing unusual had happened."[288]

An estimated $100,000 was in the train's safe at the time of the wreck. Initial reports indicate that responders did not immediately locate the safe but found it a couple of days later "red hot and unopened when found, but of course its contents were totally consumed."[289] Mailbags destined for Louisville, Cincinnati, Philadelphia and Buffalo were destroyed during the crash.

About two hours after the wreck, the Memphis-bound train, running behind schedule, approached the scene of the disaster. One of the passengers on the second train, Dr. Watkins, rendered aid to passengers. The "living dead," as the press called the severely injured survivors, were transferred to the formerly Memphis-bound train, which returned to Clarksville.

Discussing the Budds Creek crossing, an article in the *Public Ledger* stated: "It was thought to be a perfectly safe portion of the road....The remnants of timber left standing show perfectly sound."[290] Reports seemingly indicate that recent rains had weakened the bridge's foundations. Interestingly, an earlier incarnation of the bridge was burned in October 1861 and minimally damaged. It was quickly repaired and returned to service.[291]

By August 2, 1869, the L&N was paying passengers for their lost luggage. Ten or twelve trunks were delivered to the depot in Louisville, where passengers could claim their missing luggage. "Where parties have lost baggage entirely by the burning of the cars, it is necessary for them to present a sworn statement setting forth the fact that they were on the train, and specifying the several articles contained in their trunks, etc., and the values thereof, and the fact that these were destroyed or lost in consequence of the accident."[292]

The Budds Creek disaster happened in an era when railroad crashes were plentiful.[293] Because there was not yet a National Transportation Safety Board, investigators did not descend on the scene like they do today to probe what happened and render a verdict about the cause. This opened the door to rampant speculation about the cause of the wreck.

A Flow of Misinformation

The tragedy garnered a considerable number of headlines in newspapers across the country—including in Pennsylvania, Kansas and Mississippi—and even across the ocean in England. Different accounts offered varying levels of dramatic interpretation. Initial details, however, were inaccurate, and various reports misidentified those killed and injured in the crash, making it a challenge to compile a definitive account of what transpired. Some reports misidentified the location as "Rudd's Creek."

The *Louisville Evening Express*, an evening paper, published news of the disaster on its front page under the headline "DREADFUL RAILROAD ACCIDENT," in all capital letters, while the *Public Ledger* in Memphis placed a short story on page two and a more in-depth account on the next page.

Passenger Hamilton Pike, traveling with his sister, sent word to the *Memphis Daily Appeal*: "The engineer, fireman, and one other railroad official (believed to be the express agent), and one or two passengers were killed outright," he said. "About twenty-five passengers were seriously injured. Scarcely any one escaped without injury. The baggage was entirely lost. Sister and I are safe and unhurt."

The wreck might also serve as a cautionary tale for how easily inaccurate information could make it into print. Initial reports listed John C. Dugan, an Adams Express Company employee working that night as the train's express messenger, as fatally injured. A subsequent account, however, said he was badly wounded. An even later story revealed he "is not dead. He is doing well."[294]

Although Dugan survived the wreck, his condition was apparently anything but "well." In fact, the Associated Press account that said "his case is doubtful" may be the most accurate statement of the initial reports. Workers found the native of Lockport, New York, lodged beneath a car following the crash and took him to the Clarksville station, but he was so badly burned and injured that doctors apparently left him to die. However, a German man named Wenzler noticed signs of life and sent for a tub of hot water, into which he placed Dugan. Wenzler, who lived in the area, worked to remove blood clots from Dugan's throat. The German man eventually moved Dugan from the Clarksville station to his residence, where six to eight doctors worked to save the trainman.

At one point, doctors felt they would need to remove Dugan's eyes. "Mr. Dugan was helpless and could not raise his hand against them, but he told them if they did, and he recovered he would kill every one of them, as he preferred dying to [losing] his eyes," according to an Illinois Central Railroad history published in 1900. In the process, however, a leech apparently injured his right eye, causing the iris to turn back. Despite these efforts, at one point, Dugan's condition worsened, and doctors again left him to die. In fact, he was fitted for a new suit and a coffin.

But Dugan did not die. Not only did he survive, he returned to service on the railroad, where he worked as a general agent's clerk until at least 1880. He then entered into nonrailroad business but returned to the rails after some supposed friends swindled him out of money. Dugan was apparently so grateful for the German man's action that he named one of his sons in his honor. That son, Frank Wenzler Dugan, later worked as a lumber inspector in both Louisville and Memphis.[295]

The Passengers

Determining the names and hometowns of those injured in the wreck is decidedly difficult given that the spelling of passengers' and crewmembers' names varied by report. The following lists represent an attempt to name everyone who was injured and were compiled based on multiple reports.

Several people luckily walked away from the wreck without injury or relatively unharmed. Among them were M.W. Ely of Clarksville, Sam P. Rose, General Albert Pike and Captain Hamilton Pike and his sister. Mr. Doll and Mr. White also apparently escaped unharmed.

In many ways, the passenger manifest represents a "who's who" of business communities in cities across the southeast. Nolan Fontaine moved to Memphis in 1861 and was a leading merchant with the firm Fontaine, Hill & Co., the "largest inland cotton and grocery factor business in the United States and the third largest in the world."[296] Following the wreck, Fontaine, whose first name is usually spelled "Noland," returned to Memphis by August 14, 1869, while his wife remained in Louisville to recover from her injuries.[297] His home in Memphis is now the Woodruff-Fontaine House Museum.

Another passenger, J.J. Buck, was the editor of the *Patriot* newspaper in Clarksville. A native of Moscow Township, Michigan, Buck was "what might be properly called a hot-headed Abolitionist" and "an advocate of free speech." He graduated from Hillsdale College in Michigan and joined the U.S. Army, participating in Union general William T. Sherman's March to the Sea in 1864. He settled in Clarksville following his retirement from the U.S. Army. Locals initially disliked him but grew to respect him, electing him to the position of district judge. After leaving Clarksville, Buck moved to Emporia, Kansas, where he practiced law.[298]

The Cause

The record of the precise cause of the wreck is rather hazy. In the immediate aftermath, speculation was rampant, and coverage of the wreck soon dropped from newspapers' pages. However, a few probabilities rise to the top of the list:

• Defective bridge construction caused it to collapse under the weight of the train.
• A problem with the train's rolling stock (such as a broken wheel or axle) caused the train to derail and fly off the bridge, taking the structure with it.
• Some sort of vandalism, such as cutting bridge timbers or the removal of a rail before the disaster.
• Recent heavy rains that weakened the bridge's foundations, causing it to collapse.

Because there are no records of a thorough investigation, the truth is likely lost to history. It is more than possible that a combination of the aforementioned possible causes led to the disaster.

A few days after the wreck, a correspondent for the *Cincinnati Commercial*—who, coincidently, rode over the spot of the crash four days before the tragedy—returned to the scene to inspect it. "There seems to have been a systematic attempt to conceal the real facts in the case, and to set afloat fictions in their place. The facts seem to show culpability on the part of the directors of the road; the fictions seem intended to throw the responsibility anywhere but where it should rest."

In defending his position, the writer questioned many of the facts that had been printed in other publications, including whether the bridge was rebuilt following the war. The writer claimed the bridge's timbers were "water soaked, split and rotten in many places." The writer also said the bridge's timbers were made of poplar, not oak or red pine that was readily available in the area, and claimed a "reliable officer of the company" maintained the railroad's chief engineer previously reported the trestle to be unsafe. "That it did not fall before seems a miracle," the correspondent wrote, further reporting:

An exposure of the facts in this case will alone tend to prevent similar disasters. It may, for instance, compel the company to erect some more substantial work in place of that hell-trap just north of Clarksville, where there is a trestle-work a quarter of a mile long, a portion of it ninety feet high, and which is as unsubstantial, rickety, and rotten, as the spirit of mischief could desire.

Three lives have been sacrificed, more than twenty persons have been maimed, much personal baggage has been destroyed, and several mail bags of letters have been burnt up, in this midnight horror. I venture to affirm that a year will not pass by without a repetition of the disaster on this road, possibly on a more gigantic scale, unless the more treacherous of these wooden structures are superseded by others of greater strength and durability.[299]

Despite his speculation, the writer seemed unaware of the December 7, 1866 wreck in roughly the same location. Otherwise, the newspaper would have had a great conspiracy to promote in its pages. Curiously, the writer also indicated the $100,000 of specie (coins) allegedly on the train was in fact not on board at the time of the crash.

In a newspaper interview following the wreck, Conductor Matt Lowe felt the train "check up from the reduced pressure of steam as the engine approached the structure over Budd's creek." Lowe was confident the engineer was not to blame and believed the cause of the accident was defective timbers. However, an inspector had checked the bridge a few days before the wreck.[300] Lowe refuted the assertion that the train was speeding, saying the train was running its usual fifteen miles per hour for that section of track.

In September 1869, F.O. Anderson, an assistant attorney general, had summonses served on several MC&L employees, including the railroad's leadership. According to an article in the *Clarksville Tobacco Leaf*, "Railroad officers are anxious for the matter to be thoroughly investigated, believing that they will be exonerated from all blame, as the unfortunate accident, which caused the death of several and the wounding of many others, was unavoidable and not attributable to any neglect or mismanagement on their part."[301]

News reports published following the wreck pushed a narrative that some level of nefarious actions played a role in the wreck. "From conversation with railroad men here it is thought highly probable the late accident was the result of incendiarism," the *Courier-Journal* reported in a front page, above-the-fold story on an August 1, 1869. The paper further reported that unidentified soldiers and people immediately ransacked the unburned sleeping car: "They seemed to come from the woods nearby."[302]

By November 1869, following a "careful and full investigation," MC&L superintendent Robert Meek and the railroad's leadership "were entirely exonerated from all blame."[303] In May 1870, Meek testified that an "investigation made by a committee of the directors, and master builders of Clarksville, a few hours after the accident," determined "the cause of the accident was the result of a broken axle under the baggage car or front end of the bureau car." That threw the train from the track and into the ravine. Because the wreck happened on its line, the MC&L was financially liable for damages, which amounted to more than $25,000, including $11,241.91 to passengers who lost their luggage in the disaster.[304]

In 1870, a committee looking into the MC&L found defective rolling stock belonging to the Louisville & Nashville was to blame. Perhaps the true cause of the disaster is lost to history. The accounts that do exist disagree on many details, from the cause to the names of those killed and injured to the number of cars on the train (anywhere from four to seven).

The Aftermath

Days after the disaster, the Budds Creek affair remained a hot topic of conversation in Memphis. On a train arriving in Bluff City, one anonymous passenger could not wait to discuss the topic with his neighbor. "That was a terrible affair on the railroad the other night—three men killed outright and the train burned," he said, according to a report in a local newspaper. The paper did not record his neighbor's response.

In Memphis, Colonel Samuel B. Jones, the Memphis & Ohio's general superintendent, worked to secure new arrangements so service could continue as seamlessly as possible. He succeeded in routing trains via Nashville, continuing to make the railroad's planned connections with other railroads.

Meanwhile, a special train arrived at Budds Creek at 5:00 p.m. on July 28, 1869, sixteen hours after the tragedy, to pick up passengers able to travel. The railroad repaired the trestle with frightening speed, from an operational standpoint, spending $73.38 on the repairs.[305] A notice in the July 31, 1869 edition of the *Public Ledger* indicates through trains were to begin running on the Memphis & Louisville starting that day.

However, the railroad planned a larger structure across Budds Creek. It "is intended during the coming year to erect a fifty-foot truss bridge over the water-way at this point."[306] In addition to repairing the bridge, the MC&L

spent $3,475.32 to repair the locomotive involved in the Budds Creek disaster, representing nearly 10 percent of the money the railroad spent on locomotive repairs for the 1869–70 fiscal year. The locomotive returned to service and ran 20,723 miles during the year, mostly pulling passenger trains.

Even as railroad operations returned to normal, the search for what happened continued, according to an article reprinted in the *Galveston Daily News*:

> *The trestle near Clarksville, through which the train fell Tuesday night, has been repaired and the trains are running as usual. It is now believed that accident was caused by the removal of a rail or the sawing of the trestle timbers by an unknown enemy of that road. Several persons are suspected and investigations are now being made which will, if the suppositions are correct, bring the guilty parties to justice. Some of the people living in the neighborhood of the accident have been found with property in their possession belonging to the dead or wounded passengers. So it seems the bodies of the dead and wounded were robbed immediately after the accident.* [307]

It does appear there was some level of looting. On July 30, authorities arrested a "train boy" named Josh (or Joseph) Nolan. He arrived at the scene of the wreck on the second train and went into the wrecked sleeping car to procure blankets and pillows to help aid wounded passengers.

Shortly before retiring for the evening, Judge H.C. Caulkins of New Orleans, who was traveling with his wife and two children, placed his gold watch and about $1,000 in one of the "sponge pillows." When he ran into the train, Nolan grabbed the pillow containing Caulkins's watch and money, pocketing both.

Another railroad employee later saw Nolan with the watch and reported it to the judge, who confirmed the watch was indeed his. Investigators did not immediately discover the missing money. Regardless, the employee alerted railroad officials, who asked Louisville detectives Jack Gallagher and Delos T. Bligh to investigate the matter. When Nolan arrived back in Louisville, the investigators hauled him to the station to interrogate him about the missing money. At first, he denied having the money, then turned over $100, then $230 more. Nolan eventually handed over another $100. Nolan had tucked the money into the folds of his pants, necktie and collar. The remaining money was not immediately discovered, and one press account reported this was Nolan's first theft. Prior to this episode, Nolan was regarded "as an upright, honest lad, and was much esteemed by his associates on the railroad."[308]

Nolan's attorneys planned to argue he "found the money, and not knowing the owner, and presuming him dead, thought he had a right to keep it."[309] Apparently, the defense worked. Nolan appeared in Louisville's City Court on August 4, 1869. Detective Gallagher was the only witness to testify: "This evidence was altogether hearsay, and being uncorroborated by positive testimony, the prisoner was discharged."[310]

Paying Tribute

Days after the deadly wreck, on August 4, 1869, members of Division 78 of the Brotherhood of Locomotive Engineers met in Louisville and adopted a resolution in honor of engineer Eugene Riley (the organization spelled his last name "Reiley"):

WHEREAT, It is with heartfelt sorrow and regret that we are called upon to announce the melancholy death of our worthy Brother, Eugene Reiley, who was killed in the discharge of his duty as Engineer, July 28, 1869, at about 1 o'clock, a. m., on the Clarksville Division of the Memphis & Louisville Railroad by his Engine breaking through Budds Creek Bridge. Therefore, be it

Resolved, That we bow in humble submission to that allwise Being acknowledging that unto him we are indebted for every good and perfect gift, that we realize in our bereavement the paramount duty of all flesh that of so living, that when our Heavenly Father shall summon us home, we shall go in peace.

Resolved, That to the relatives of deceased and to the bereaved Widow and Children we tender our [heartfelt] sympathy in their hour of sorrow; and for consolation commend them to Him who is the giver of all good; and may they meet in that boundless realm, where the loved ones know no parting.

Resolved, That as a token of respect to the memory of our deceased Brother, our Engines shall be draped in mourning for ten days, and that we wear the usual badge for thirty days, and that a copy with seal of Division attached, be presented [to] the family, and be published in the [Courier] Journal, and Locomotive Engineers' Journal.

Riley's sister, Maggie E. Riley of Ypsilanti, Michigan, penned the following poem in honor of her late brother:

We have given him up
To He who reigns on high,
And the many friends who mourn his loss
Remember he said he was prepared to die.

Yes, Death has robbed us of our brother,
And he's joined the angels now,
Where no trouble, pain or sorrow
Goes to cloud his darling brow.

And the long years of future though death has parted
The affection so fervent and strong;
Oh! we sigh, yes, sigh deeply
When we think of our loved brother who's gone.

Ah! the sting of his death almost killed us,
It has broken the hearts of us all;
It has taken one of the fondest and truest,
Who's [sic] place can never be filled.

Yes, gone from us forever,
No more his bright smile we will see;
His heart-broken wife and two children,
How lonely, how lonely they'll be.

We weep as we had not wept for years—
Since our dear, dear mother before him had gone;
But God knows best who to choose
To make their homes with Him.

Years had parted us from our loved one,
He had wandered far and wide;
But in dreams I often saw him,
Even just before he died.

Every day some bright flower is plucked from its sunny home,
Yes, thou hast left us our darling,
Angel one we loved so well,
In another clime to dwell.

Parting words were not spoken,
And your dear, dear voice to us was still;
But your loving smile is with us,
Thoughts of you our bosoms fill.

The tributes continued in New Orleans, where, on September 6, 1869, the city's chamber of commerce passed a resolution honoring local merchant Hugh McColl:

Whereas, this body has learned of the death of Mr. HUGH McCOLL, under circumstances of peculiar sadness, and

Whereas, an [expression] of the sorrow thus occasioned is a tribute most justly due from those whose social and business relations with the deceased have been so painfully sundered. it is hereby

Resolved, That the Chamber of Commerce would in any event have experienced heartfelt regret at the death of a member so truly honored as HUGH McCOLL, and the regret is deepened by a knowledge of the distressing circumstances under which his life ended.

Resolved, That we cherish and value the memory of HUGH McCOLL as that of a courteous, just and upright gentleman, a citizen of worth and usefulness, and a merchant who by his high character lent honor and dignity to commerce.

Resolved, That our warmest sympathies are tendered to the surviving members of the family, in whose bereavement we share.

Resolved, That a copy of these resolutions be transmitted by the Secretary to the family of the deceased.

ARTHUR C. WAUGH,
Sec'y and Treas'r C. C.[311]

The local press seemingly moved on from the disaster rather quickly, offering small snippets as updates. "We are glad to learn that J.J. Buck, of the *Patriot*, who was injured in the railroad accident of the 28th inst., is rapidly recovering," the *Clarksville Chronicle* reported on July 31, 1869.[312] "We are glad to learn that the sufferers by the late railroad disaster are all getting along very well," the *Clarksville Chronicle* reported on August 7, 1869.[313]

Barely a month removed from the Budds Creek wreck, on August 31, 1869, a Memphis, Clarksville & Louisville freight train with twenty-two cars in tow "fell through" a trestle south of Humbolt, roughly half-way between Paris and Memphis, killing the fireman and a brakeman.[314] "This road has suffered wonderfully, and it seems as if this and accidents similar must be the result of villainy in cutting the timbers," declared the *Nashville Union and American*.[315]

Not unlike modern-day mishaps, the Budds Creek calamity resulted in various lawsuits, including one from J.J. Buck against the L&N seeking $10,000 in damages for his injuries. A ten-day trial in 1874 ended in a mistrial, with the jury divided six to six.[316] A Louisville bank also filed suit over money it lost in the wreck. However, like so many stories, the Budds Creek railroad disaster eventually faded from the pages of newspapers.

8

A New Hope

The deadly Budds Creek wreck notwithstanding, rather steady operations under the control of the Louisville & Nashville did little to change the railroad's financial condition, and it continued to worsen. G.A. Henry took control of the railroad starting December 1, 1869, "by giving bond to the amount of $100,000,"[317] succeeding D.B. Cliffe, whose tenure as the railroad's receiver ended on November 30, 1869.

The action seemed to give new hope for the road, as evidenced by a poem published in the *Clarksville Tobacco Leaf* in early January 1870:

> *The Railroad is turned from the terrible Cliff*
> *O'er which it was hastily rushing adrift*
> *With its sleek hunting dogs, from a system of venery,*
> *It now is transposed to A. No. 1, Henry.*
> *Yes turned from distress, by a Post-on the track,*
> *It will now to its halcyon days wander back;*
> *And the Fax-on the case will soon easily show,*
> *That e'en without 'Cash a Railroad can go.*
> *Though sifted and scattered, our Breed still abides,*
> *And with Meek (s) satisfaction our little King rides.*[318]

This rhyme certainly name-dropped, referencing not just G.A. Henry but also secretary George B. Faxon, superintendent Robert Meek and auditor and general freight agent G.C. Breed. According to *Ashcroft's Railway Directory*

90

[EXHIBIT A.]

STATEMENT OF RECEIPTS AND DISBURSEMENTS

Made by G. A. HENRY, Receiver of the Memphis, Clarksville and Louisville Railroad, from December 1, 1869, to April 1, 1870.

RECEIPTS.

Amount received from Passengers transported		$ 60,292 42	
" " " Freight "		69,304 77	
" " " Express Companies		4,840 00	
Total		$134,437 19	

DISBURSEMENTS.

Stock on hand not paid for*	$ 20,000 00	
MISCELLANEOUS.		
Improvement account, (new work)	3,627 10	
EQUIPMENT.		
For Depot Repairs	208 17	
" Water Station Repairs	667 42	
" Section House Repairs	99 33	
MAINTENANCE OF WAY.		
For Road Repairs	22,734 00	
" General Expense of Road	759 94	
" Repairs of Bridges	19,226 56	
MOTIVE POWER.		
For Fuel	12,077 90	
" Water Supply	1,343 65	
" Motive Power	9,686 47	
" Repairs of Locomotives	8,393 49	
" General Expense Machinery	2,751 03	
TRANSPORTATION.		
For Depot Furniture	59 37	
" Stationery and Printing	682 30	
" Advertising	1,478 87	
" Injury to Persons	150 00	
" Loss and Damage on Goods	560 81	

*This stock is composed of wood, ties and timber on road; also, material for cars and engines in Machine Shop, which is charged to the different accounts only as it is used; and said material has been paid for by the Memphis, Clarksville and Nashville Railroad; and this Nashville Railroad now in existence, is bound to pay for this material; and no surplus will be paid to the Receiver by the Louisville and Nashville Railroad until there is a surplus over and above the amount necessary to pay for material on the road.

91

[EXHIBIT A.—DISBURSEMENTS—*Continued.*]

For Stock Killed or Injured	$ 485 00	
" Train Expenses	338 95	
" Wages of Conductors and Train Men	7,877 98	
" Wages of Agents and Clerks	6,833 66	
" Station Labor	818 84	
" Telegraph Expenses	1,574 56	
" Mileage	7,559 06	
" Station Expenses	672 21	
" Watchmen—Road	2,043 93	
MAINTENANCE OF CARS.		
For Passenger Car Repairs	12 01	
" Freight Car Repairs	3,109 91	
" Oil and waste	1,421 25	
GENERAL EXPENSES.		
For Gratuity to Employes	385 98	
" Attorney's Fees	200 00	
" Incidentals, General Expense	1,937 66	
" Watchmen and Switchmen	784 45	
Total	$140,561 86	

I, G. A. Henry, Receiver and President, certify that the above is a true and correct statement of the receipts and disbursements, made by me, as Receiver of the Memphis, Clarksville and Louisville Railroad, from December 1, 1869, to April 1, 1870.

G. A. HENRY, *Receiver and President.*

G.A. Henry compiled this statement of receipts and disbursements for the MC&L from December 1, 1869, to April 1, 1870. It was published in a June 1870 report of a Joint Select Committee investigating the affairs of railroads in Tennessee and submitted to the second session of the Thirty-Sixth General Assembly. *Tennessee State Library & Archives.*

for 1870–71, the MC&L had five passenger cars and eighty freight cars. The railroad's officers included a few familiar names:

President G.A. Henry
Secretary George B. Faxon
Auditor and General Freight & Ticket Agent J.C. Breed [presumably a
  misspelling of G.C. Breed]
Superintendent Robert Meek
Master of Machinery F. A. Bissett
Master of Car Repairs John Posey
Road Master Edward Partridge

The railroad's fourteen directors were W.M. Finley, R.W. Humphreys, N.L. Thomas, Jno. F. House, J.G. Hornberger, Geo. W. Hillman, W.P. Hume, Joshua Cobb, W.A. Quarles, T.W. King, James E. Rice, G.A. Henry, J.H. Porter and Joshua Elder.

Joshua Cobb (1809–1879), a graduate of the U.S. Military Academy (West Point), "was noted for his practical business sense, as well as his medical skill and thoroughly trained mind, and success attended his efforts," according to historian William P. Titus. *HathiTrust*.

Catchy ditties, however, did not carry capital with them. By July 1, 1870, the railroad's indebtedness to the L&N had risen to a total of $99,842.20.[319]

Under the control of the L&N, the railroad conducted extensive repairs. This work included ballasting 67,670 linear feet of track with 21,962 yards of gravel. While twenty miles of the road were ballasted, sixty-three miles still needed ballast. Crews placed 41,141 new crossties and laid 171 tons of "new iron" along the route. By this point, the railroad considered all bridges and trestles to be in satisfactory condition. These improvements allowed the railroad to increase the speed of its trains from 17 miles per hour to 23 miles per hour.[320]

During this same period, the railroad operated over a total of 233,364 train miles, including 107,460 passenger train miles, 90,009 freight train miles and 35,895 for other service.[321] The railroad was maintaining its rolling stock, but Robert Meek, superintendent of the MC&L, estimated the railroad would need five new locomotives, four passenger coaches, two baggage cars and one hundred freight cars to handle "the business of this road."

Despite the work the L&N did on the road after taking it over on February 17, 1868, much work remained to be done. Management planned to re-lay eight miles of track between Clarksville and the state line and lengthen a pair of sidings.

Earnings for this time were improving, as the railroad reported a 33 percent increase for the year ending June 30, 1868, but they remained sluggish.[322]

TABLE 4
According to the 1869–70 Louisville & Nashville annual report, the
Memphis, Clarksville & Louisville reported the following earnings:

Month	Total
March 1868	$18,641.38
April 1868	$18,501.42
May 1868	$15,664.50
June 1868	$18,452.35
July 1868	$20,160.02
August 1868	$22,157.05
September 1868	$27,747.53
October 1868	$26,655.05
November 1868	$24,252.08
December 1868	$27,894.81
January 1869	$27,148.48
February 1869	$30,000.56
March 1869	$31,229.78
April 1869	$25,653.92
May 1869	$22,374.33
June 1869	$22,713.65

Regardless, the outlook for the railroad was dire. For the year ending on June 30, 1869, the railroad had $313,940.81 in operating expenses against $307,987.26 in earnings. That left $5,953.55 in expenses above earnings.

TRAGEDY CONTINUES

Around 4:00 p.m. on February 10, 1870, locomotive No. 9, a Norris & Son–built 4-4-0 steamer, was pulling a freight train over the Red River trestle roughly one mile from Clarksville. Since July 1, 1869, the railroad had used the steamer exclusively for its freight service, running it for a total of 17,431 miles in service during that timeframe. As it was pulling the freight train on this particular Thursday, the locomotive's boiler suddenly exploded.

The blast sent engineer Thomas J. Bradley "whizzing through the air for some distance" into a telegraph wire, nearly severing his body in half.[323] Firemen Thomas Campin and Jonathan Cousins "were found, bruised and bleeding, beneath the fragments of the wreck, and conveyed to the National Hotel, where the best of medical attention was rendered to alleviate their intense suffering, but all was in vain....They were gathered in the cold embrace of death at a late hour that night."[324]

Bradley, who was also the master mechanic at the railroad's shops in Clarksville, left behind a wife, while Cousins, a resident of Providence, Tennessee, left behind a wife and two children. "We have not learned the cause of this dreadful explosion—or whether the cause can be laid at any one's door—which has cast a gloom over the hearts of so many of our citizens," declared one newspaper account.[325]

A few months later, the *Clarksville Chronicle* reported on July 30, 1870, that in yet another misfortune, a "quantity of dirt and stone caved into the Palmyra tunnel, from the top, but the energetic Superintendent, Mr. Meek, had it removed so speedily that the trains passed through the next day."

State Review

In mid-1870, a special committee looked into the Memphis, Clarksville & Louisville. At this time, the railroad had eleven locomotives, sixty-eight boxcars and three condemned passenger cars. A committee report also found the company still owed George T. Lewis $1,170 for his services leading the company.[326] As part of its findings, the committee found:

First, To the fact that the bonds issued to said road and drawn by the Receiver, were sold or exchanged at less than par.

Second, To the large salaries drawn or retained by the Receivers—particularly to the amount retained by S. B. Brown, which, in the opinion of the committee—derived from the testimony—was the result of a conspiracy entered into between a set of politicians to swindle the State, and by which the State lost about $6,000, in that particular transaction.

Third, To the Act of February 1, 1861, which is the only law the committee have been able to find regulating the salaries of Receivers, and which, in but few instances, has been complied with.

Fourth, To the fact that said road as been operated for more than two years under one management, as a part of the through line between Louisville and Memphis, at the same time being a necessary and important connecting link in the through line from New York to New Orleans, and has failed to produce any earnings over and above its necessary expenses, as appears from testimony, while other connecting roads in the through line have made large earnings.

Fifth, To the hardship to said road under the contract, as construed by the Louisville and Nashville Railroad Company, by which the Memphis, Clarksville and Louisville Railroad Company is held responsible for all loss or damage sustained from accidents occurring on their bed, when—as appears from the testimony in regard to the "Budd's Creek Disaster"—said disaster was caused by defective rolling stock belonging to the Louisville and Nashville Railroad Company, and for which the Louisville and Nashville Railroad has charged the Memphis, Clarksville and Louisville Railroad between $25,000 and $30,000, for loss and damage, paid on account of said disaster.[327]

The real news was that the committee recommended the state legislature either sell the line or appoint a state official with authority to make an "equitable consolidated running arrangement" with its connecting railroads—the Memphis & Ohio and the L&N. As a part of the equitable consolidated running arrangement, the officer would confirm the MC&L received appropriate proceeds for its services. The committee also wanted the appointed state official to investigate former receiver S.B. Brown's excessive salary.

END OF THE LINE

Interestingly, in 1870, the railroad's finances looked as if they were improving.

"Those who have no confidence in the Memphis, Clarksville and Louisville Railroad, and want it incontinently sold out, and our county and municipal hands washed of the whole thing will discover…that the road is in good condition," stated the *Clarksville Tobacco Leaf*. "This road should, by all means, be preserved to us. It is a valuable road, and as an adjunct to another road, and in the hands of its own company, it will be of great advantage to us in the development of our country—our section of Kentucky and Tennessee."[328]

Table 5
According to 1869–70 Louisville & Nashville annual report, Memphis,
Clarksville & Louisville locomotive miles operated the following miles
for 1870:

Number	Mileage with Trains				
	Passenger	Freight	Distributing	Total	Total Repairs and Running Expenses
1	804	5,515	19,750	26,069	$4,728.86
2	975	14,210	4,604	19,789	$3,386.23
3	19,174	12,547	0	31,721	$6,664.85
4	27,471	8,355	0	35,826	$5,095.86
5	4,829	10,013	8,458	23,300	$3,541.11
6	0	5,617	5,577	11,194	$7,140.53
7	65	28,125	0	28,190	$5,648.35
8	0	15,612	1,900	17,512	$5,248.25
9	0	17,431	0	17,431	$3,381.67
10	32,678	356	0	33,034	$5,394.27
11	13,222	7,392	170	20,784	$8,019.26
12	34,241	0	0	34,241	$7,129.35
Repairs of L&N engine wrecked at Budds Creek					$3,475.32
TOTAL	133,459	125,173	40,459	299,091	$68,853.91

TABLE 6
According to a report in the *Clarksville Tobacco Leaf* on December 14, 1870, the Memphis, Clarksville & Louisville reported the following earnings. [Note: The numbers have been reproduced from the original but do not tally.]

	Earnings	Expenses
December 1869	$37,896.61	$28,614.18
January 1870	$32,434.01	$32,104.38
Feburary 1870	$29,950.63	$28,941.32
March 1870	$34,847.71	$30,002.03
April 1870	$31,210.60	$30,598.51
May 1870	$29,173.84	$30,608.74
June 1870	$28,013.58	$30,086.06
July 1870	$30,130.27	$32,430.61
August 1870	$34,466.04	$33,412.90
September 1870	$48,825.89	$33,407.40
October 1870 (approximately)	$52,533.76	$34,000.00
TOTAL	$389,521.95	$351,106.06

Concurrently, fairly significant improvements continued, including extensions to a siding in Guthrie and a new water station in Clarksville.

Regardless, it increasingly looked as if the company's leaders would sell the route. As a result, the railroad's creditors filed for an injunction against its sale.[329] But, just as it had so many times before, the railroad's operations continued.

In January 1871, Robert Meek oversaw a number of repairs around the depot, including the construction of a new turntable, the addition of gravel to the tracks, new crossties and new rails. The railroad also built a separate waiting room for black passengers—a sign of the times. "The traveling community, both white and black, will fully appreciate this additional feature of comfort and convenience," claimed the *Clarksville Chronicle*.[330]

On May 20, 1871, stockholders gathered to elect new officers and board members. While there were some familiar names, eight directors were new: G.A. Henry, William A. Quarles, Robert W. Humphreys, T.W. King, John F. House, W.M. Daniel, H.H. Lurton, D.N. Kennedy, B.W. Macrae, B.O.

80

STATEMENT OF RECEIPTS AND DISBURSEMENTS.

Made by D. B. Cliffe, Receiver of the Memphis, Clarksville and Louisville Railroad, from January 22, 1868, to December 1, 1870.

RECEIPTS.

Amount received from Passengers transported........	$ 276,010 80
" " " Freight "	284,943 86
" " " Express Companies.............	21,538 23
" " " Rents and Privileges............	298 34
FROM OTHER SOURCES.	
Material Account, (sold and used)......................	2,954 95
Individual Assets.......................	142 09
Material sold Louisville and Nashville Railroad......	20,285 30
Due " " "	2,667 41
Total...................................	$608,840 98

DISBURSEMENTS.

MISCELLANEOUS.	
F. W. Palmer, Agent......................	$ 1,111 80
Capt. S. B. Brown's Administration....................	13,314 52
Amount paid on account former Receiver or R. R. Co	21 51
For Internal Revenue, County and State Tax.........	2 00
" Improvement Account, (new work).................	20,484 14
EQUIPMENT.	
Due from Agents........................	2,267 98
NEW BUILDINGS.	
For Shops and Engine Houses......................	224 47
For Freight and Passenger Houses, (repairs)..........	1,423 59
For Water Stations,	2,589 59
" Section House, "	337 55
CONSTRUCTION.	
For Engineering..................................	62 00
MAINTENANCE OF WAY.	
For Masonry................................	1,050 42
For Repairs of Bridges and Trestle......................	62,436 26
For Watching Bridges and Trestle......................	8,576 37
For Expense of Road........................	4,025 17
" Ballast..................................	3,093 51
" Road Repairs...............................	114,650 42

81

STATEMENT.—*Continued.*

MOTIVE POWER.	
For Fuel..................................	36,910 85
" Water Supply......................	6,432 72
" General Expense Machinery........................	10,598 83
" Repairs of Locomotives................................	54,745 10
" Individual Accounts................................	289 60
" Motive Power................................	40,110 09
TRANSPORTATION.	
For Lost Baggage........................	11,241 91
" Stationery and Printing................................	5,139 39
" Printing and Advertising................................	9,012 74
" Injury to Persons................................	3,835 44
" Loss, Damage and Over-charge on Goods..........	1,506 42
" Stock Killed or Injured................................	782 82
" Train Expenses................................	2,518 40
" Wages of Conductors and Train Men..............	35,431 70
" Wages of Agents and Clerks........................	36,108 62
" Station Labor................................	4,768 64
" Gratuity to Employes................................	1,357 25
" Mileage................................	41,317 55
" Station Expenses................................	4,473 82
" Watchmen and Switchmen................................	3,319 41
" Telegraph Repairs................................	34 25
MAINTENANCE OF CARS.	
For Oil, Tallow and Waste........................	4,536 21
" Wages—Machinist and Laborers.................	13,169 48
" Passenger Car Repairs........................	106 82
" For Incidentals........................	19,683 55
" Freight Car Repairs........................	14,187 22
GENERAL EXPENSES.	
For Salaries................................	2,240 84
" Attorney's Fees................................	
" Incidentals................................	710 00
" Depot Furniture................................	134 73
" Telegraph Expenses................................	8,465 28
Total................................	$608,840 98

I, D. B. CLIFFE, Receiver of the Memphis, Clarksville and Louisville Railroad, certify that the above is a true and correct statement of the Receipts and Disbursements, made by me as Receiver of the Memphis, Clarksville and Louisville Railroad, from January 22, 1868, to December 1, 1869, to the best of my knowledge and belief.
D. B. CLIFFE.

6 M.C.&L.R.R.

Receiver D.B. Cliffe compiled this statement of receipts and disbursements for the MC&L from January 22, 1868, to December 1, 1869. It was published in a June 1870 report of a Joint Select Committee investigating the affairs of railroads in Tennessee and submitted to the second session of the Thirty-Sixth General Assembly. *Tennessee State Library & Archives.*

Keesee, H. F. Cummins, J.E. Bailey, Joshua Elder and H.C. Merritt. A few days later, on May 25, 1871, Henry was reelected as president, and George B. Faxon was reelected as secretary and treasurer.[331] These were the railroad's last elected leaders.

When the L&N leased the MC&L in 1868, it not only supported it financially, it also helped improve its infrastructure. Despite the improvements, however, the MC&L wasn't able to operate self-sufficiently, and the movement to sell the road continued. In April 1871, the legal argument about whether the road could be sold was still ongoing, but no decision was immediately rendered.[332]

A few months later, in July 1871, a judge ordered that the road be sold for $1.7 million. "The Chancellor held in the cause that the second mortgage bonds were subsequent in lien to the whole of the States debt, both to that issued before and since the execution of the mortgage by the company," according to a report in the *Republican Banner*.[333]

The MC&L's end came in October 1871, when the L&N purchased it. When it subsumed the MC&L, the L&N added the MC&L's assets, including its tracks between the Tennessee-Kentucky state line and Paris and eleven locomotives.

To finance construction of the railroad during the 1850s, officials raised more than $2 million in capital. Montgomery County, the city of Clarksville, Henry County and individuals gave monetary support to the railroad. The State of Tennessee supported the railroad with $10,000 per mile. In July 1871, a chancery court judge ruled that the MC&L could be sold for $1.7 million.

A September 20, 1871 decree held: "the State will indemnify and save harmless the purchaser from liability for the debt to the United States…less the amount due from the United States, up to the time of sale, for carrying the mails or other freight, of which the State is to have the benefit."[334]

In October 1871, the L&N formally began executing its purchase of the MC&L. The *Republican Banner* reported that the L&N "paid into the hands of the Comptroller" $750,000 in bonds as the first payment for the MC&L. The newspaper's report stated: "We understand that the remaining portion of the $1,700,000, the price at which the State's interest in the road was purchased, will be held in reserve until the matters between the road and the Government shall have been adjusted."[335]

What were previously locomotives numbered 1 through 12 on the MC&L were renumbered as locomotive numbers 201 through 212 on the L&N, though the steamers were not long for the railroad world.[336]

A year after the sale, the L&N said the MC&L was worth at least $2 million.[337] The purchase signaled the beginning of a roughly 115-year-long run of the Memphis Branch being operated by the L&N and its successor lines.

Table 7

When the Louisville & Nashville assumed the Memphis, Clarksville & Louisville, it renumbered its locomotives. Here are the new road numbers and their ultimate disposition, according to the 1869–70 Louisville & Nashville annual report and historian Richard E. Prince:

MC&L Number	L&N Number	No. of Drivers	Size of Drivers (inches)	Size of Cylinder	Builder	Disposition
1	201	4	54	14x22	Danforth, Cooke & Co.	Scrapped in 1876
2	202	4	47	14x22	Danforth, Cooke & Co.	Sold in 1878
3	203	4	54	15x24	Hinkley	Rebuilt in 1872
4	204	4	56	15x24	Hinkley	Scrapped in 1876
5	205	4	56	15x22	Norris & Son	Scrapped in 1876
6	206	4	54	16x24	Norris & Son	(unknown)
7	207	4	57	16x24	Norris & Son	Sold in 1881
8	208	4	60	16x24	Norris & Son	Rebuilt in 1875
9	n/a	4	60	16x24	Norris & Son	Destroyed in February 1870
10	210	4	60	15x24	Baldwin Locomotive Works	Scrapped in 1876
11	211	4	58	15x24	Baldwin Locomotive Works	Scrapped in 1885
12	212	4	58	15x24	Baldwin Locomotive Works	Scrapped in 1885

THE HOLLOW TREE

In May 1881, roughly a decade after the Louisville & Nashville fully subsumed the Memphis, Clarksville & Louisville, former MC&L officers gathered in Clarksville for a reunion. The group "revived the memories of the past; we have renewed the friendships formed in the days of our youth" and "mingled together in delightful companionship and mutual sympathy and goodwill."[338] The reunion included a tour of hotspots throughout the city, a banquet at the Tobacco Exchange and "a grand hop" featuring a "fine string band."

"This will be the hop of the season, and it is hoped all the ladies and gentlemen will turn out in full force," the *Clarksville Weekly Chronicle* reported.[339] It was a moment of celebration for a railroad that seemed to have nothing but difficulties during its operational life.

Newspapers played up the soirée, and by all accounts, it was quite the bash. G.A. Roth, "the prince of caterers" (as the *Clarksville Tobacco Leaf* put it), catered the event held at the Tobacco Exchange building. Attendees enjoyed an extensive menu, including "Broiled Potomac Shad with Cream Potato" and "Spring Chickens with Asparagus and Lobster Salad."[340] This was quite the spread for a railroad that stretched over just eighty-three miles, operated for slightly longer than a decade—much of that time in receivership—and was decidedly something less than a money-printing press.

Regardless, attendees represented a "who's who" of railroad leaders, including Gilbert C. Breed, a former engineer; William A. Quarles, a former president; George B. Fleece, a former chief engineer; George B. Faxon, a

John F. House (1827–1904) served in a number of public roles. In his obituary, the *Nashville American* wrote that the state had lost "one of her best citizens, ablest men and most worthy sons." *HathiTrust*.

former treasurer and secretary; and John F. House, a former board member. "The programme was carried out in the smallest particulars, and nothing was left undone or said, to make the occasion one of unalloyed pleasure and enjoyment," the *Clarksville Weekly Chronicle* noted.[341]

In writing "The Ante-Bellum History of the M. C. & L. Railroad Company" for the *Louisville Courier Journal* (subsequently republished in the *Clarksville Weekly Chronicle* on May 28, 1881), John W. Faxon, a prominent Clarksville citizen, remarked:

> *The road was, from its inception, an elephant on the hands of the company on account of its length—eighty-three miles. Even if the war had not [interfered] with its running arrangements, it never would have paid a dollar dividend on the amount invested, and for this reason, if for none other, it was a wise stroke of policy to dispose of it to the Louisville and Nashville railroad.*[342]

The May 1881 gathering more than likely was the last positive event associated with the railroad. For the county, the matter was not settled, and selling the MC&L did not end Clarksville's or Montgomery County's financial connection to the railroad. Its impact on the county—and, particularly, its finances—reverberated for decades.

During this same time, a party that claimed it paid "large sums" to help build the MC&L filed suit against Montgomery County. The railroad never reimbursed this party, and the party argued that its claim had a greater priority than that of any stockholder. The suit dragged on for six years before it was "compromised."[343] In 1875, Chancellor Cooper ruled in favor of Montgomery County. In March 1878, the Tennessee Supreme Court upheld Cooper's decision.[344]

Even after the L&N subsumed the MC&L, lawsuits kept the railroad alive—at least in the courts. In one such case, a few landowners sued the MC&L, saying they were "unable to agree in the accuracy...in account of the running" of the railroad over their lands. The lawsuit dragged on for two years, and the parties agreed to appoint a surveyor to determine damages, which at one point amounted to $200, including $80 for the two acres and $120 in damages.[345] After 1895, the railroad seemingly faded into obscurity and thereafter received little to no ink in local newspapers.

LOOSE ENDS

Despite the sale, the Memphis, Clarksville & Louisville left a number of loose ends in its wake. The matter of railroad indebtedness hung over Montgomery County for years. Following the Civil War, county leaders worked to keep the debt from further ballooning, making annual levies for railroad purposes and to keep down interest. A financial report published in the February 23, 1872 edition of the *Clarksville Tobacco Leaf* addressed selling the road's bonds to the L&N to limit the detrimental impact the MC&L's legacy would leave on the local community.

The county implemented a privilege tax for railroad purposes. "Unfortunately, however, these levies were not collected, or if collected were not accounted for as required by law," Judge Charles W. Tyler noted in 1890.[346]

By 1873, the county was behind on its interest obligations, "while unpaid judgments and other demands to a large amount were outstanding against her." The county's debt in 1873 totaled $346,632.98. Some citizens tried to leave the county and unsuccessfully sought annexation by neighboring Robertson County in order to avoid repaying the debt.

By 1895, some residents, including D.N. Kennedy, a former MC&L official, wanted the county to stop collecting taxes "for railroad purposes"

Judge Charles W. Tyler (1839–1920) was highly regarded for how he handled the financial affairs of Montgomery County during the latter half of the nineteenth century. "He lived a long life, a useful life," read his obituary in the *Clarksville Leaf-Chronicle*; "Montgomery County is much richer by reason of the life and service of this splendid man." *HathiTrust*.

and filed suit against the county.[347] The county dedicated some of the revenues from the railroad tax for nonrailroad purposes, such as repairing the county courthouse.

The case made it to the Tennessee Supreme Court, which ruled in 1897: "When the people consent to be taxed for any purpose they cannot complain; but when they are taxed for one purpose and the fund applied to another, and when they are misled as to the purposes for which they are being taxed, they have a right not only to complain, but a remedy to redress the grievance, if they apply to the courts in the proper way and at the proper time." Because taxpayers waited too long to file suit, the tax stood on a technicality.

A Federal Case

Perhaps no loose end was bigger than the $340,000 the federal government claimed the state owed for rolling stock the Memphis, Clarksville & Louisville purchased after the Civil War—and seven years of interest.[348] The MC&L was one of fifty railroads that paid the federal government more than $5.6 million (combined) for rolling stock after the war. Following the passage of various bills in Congress, many railroads repaid the federal government. However, it does not appear the MC&L did.[349]

For their part, state officials contended the federal government owed them more than $600,000 for damages done to the Winchester & Alabama Railroad, a small line located west of Chattanooga. In a message, Tennessee governor John C. Brown said:

> *When the last mentioned road was sold by the Commissioners this claim became the property of and now belongs to the State. There is no authority under existing laws for the appointment of an agent to adjust these claims. The attorney employed by the Memphis, Clarksville & Louisville Railroad Company can not make a final settlement with the departments, because not accredited by this State. I deem it important that a speedy settlement of these and all other claims with the Government be made, and I respectfully request legislation authorizing the appointment of agents for this purpose.*[350]

The MC&L specifically presented a claim for $232,166.48 against the federal government for using the road during the war and also for taking and destroying property during the conflict. The office of the U.S. Army's quartermaster general denied the claim. In a July 3, 1872 letter, U.S. Army quartermaster general Brevet Major-General Andrew B. Martin wrote the claim "has been disallowed by this office for the reason that the road and property belonging to it were captured from a public enemy and thereupon became the property of the United States, so as to relieve it from all charges for its use and destruction."

Congress voted to settle the $340,000 claim, but by 1924, it apparently had not been resolved. The 1901–2 comptroller's report from the State of Tennessee revealed that $400,000—the L&N's last payment for the MC&L—in bonds were deposited in a Nashville bank. The bonds were "to be held by said bank until the State can effect a settlement with the United States."

In a December 1, 1926 report, Tennessee state treasurer Hill McAlister noted: "There is no immediate prospect of a final adjustment of either of these disputed claims." John J. Vertrees, the last of three commissioners appointed by Tennessee leaders to represent the state in its dispute with the federal government, died on July 17, 1931, with the issue not yet resolved. In a December 1, 1932 report, McAlister wrote: "A number of times before [Vertrees's] death I went over the matters in dispute between the State and the Federal Government, and it was his opinion that there was no immediate prospect of any adjustment of these disputed claims."

LIFE AFTER THE CLARKSVILLE

Buying a railroad is nothing more than a business transaction once a community's emotional attachments are removed. No matter the community's connection to a line, if it doesn't make money, the community's options are limited. Because of the Memphis, Clarksville & Louisville's vital place in connecting Louisville and Memphis, the Louisville & Nashville viewed it as a prime acquisition. After taking control of the MC&L, the L&N upgraded the line and formally merged it into its operations.

While the MC&L name faded, its route remained an important part of the L&N's Memphis Branch until the 1980s. Even after the L&N purchased the line, many newspaper accounts still referred to the tracks through Clarksville as the MC&L. Even today, the single most identifiable railroad structure in Clarksville is the Cumberland River bridge. Second on the list is the L&N Depot at Tenth and Commerce Streets.

In 1881, the L&N received proposals for a new railroad depot to be located near Bradley's Brickyard on Commerce Street. The new depot was one of many infrastructure upgrades the L&N made to the former MC&L. A fire "seriously damaged" the new depot in August 1901. It started in a waiting room closet on the building's eastern side. "Owing to the way the building had been constructed, it was one of the hardest fires to fight that the department has had to contend with for some time," according to a report in the *Daily Tobacco Leaf–Chronicle*.[351]

Passengers departing on the 6:15 a.m. train had to purchase tickets on the train, as the fire apparently caused a great deal of confusion. However, the ticket booth was back in business for the 9:20 a.m. train.

Grange Warehouse, pictured here around 1971, was originally built near the railroad around 1859 and covers three acres. From 1876 until the early twentieth century, it was the largest tobacco warehouse in the world. *Library of Congress.*

Ten years later, in 1891, the L&N rebuilt the bridge over the Cumberland River to accommodate larger locomotives. "Business is lively around the freight depot now," the *Daily Tobacco Leaf–Chronicle* reported. "The tobacco receipts are large and the hands kept pretty busy unloading."[352]

HISTORY REPEATS ITSELF

In the early 1880s, a proposal emerged for a second railroad to run from Mobile, Alabama, to Evansville, Indiana. The railroad had a confusing corporate history. Even though some paperwork was filed earlier, the Indiana, Alabama & Texas Railroad Company formed in July 1885 after the merging together of three lines:

- The Mobile, Clarksville & Evansville incorporated in late 1881 in Tennessee to build from the Tennessee-Kentucky line to the Tennessee-Alabama line north of Florence, Alabama.

- The Princeton & Ohio River Railroad incorporated in February 1882 to build from to Princeton, Kentucky, to a point on the Ohio River near the mouth of the Green River.
- The Indiana, Alabama & Texas formed in either October 1881 or February 1882 in Alabama to run from Mobile, Alabama, to the Alabama-Tennessee state line.

In Tennessee, Mobile, Clarksville & Evansville organizers sought funding from Montgomery County and the City of Clarksville to construct its line. Some of the same people who, years earlier, were instrumental in building the MC&L returned to their railroad roots and helped bring a new road to life. Two decades earlier, D.N. Kennedy declined the position of MC&L president. However, this time around, he accepted a similar role with the new Mobile, Clarksville & Evansville. Railroad proponents also elected H.C. Merritt as its secretary and treasurer. At the same time, Judge C.G. Smith of Clarksville successfully motioned to set the capital stock at $2.5 million. Individual shares were fixed at $100.

The February 25, 1882 edition of the *Clarksville Weekly Chronicle* indicated railroad officials "are now vigorously at work all along the line getting up their subscriptions." The same article predicted the road would be up and running by March 1, 1883, and lauded the railroad. "The people who possess such a spirit of enterprise will always succeed," the reporter wrote, offering a similar excitement as the papers did three decades earlier, when workers built the MC&L.

> *Nothing will save this country from utter ruin but railroads, manufactories, and a new system of farming. We must get out of old ruts. It is a shame and disgrace to our people that there is so little enterprise and so much selfishness among them. This selfishness is eating out the very life and soul of the country and the people. We must get out of it.*[353]

The *Clarksville Weekly Chronicle* reported that the city of Clarksville raised $60,000 for its subscription to the railroad. According to the paper, other cities, such as Princeton, Kentucky, would also complete the subscription fee of $30,000. But not all was certain in terms of funding for the road. As a result, the company constructed a poorly built three-foot-gauge line.

The L&N purchased the Indiana, Alabama & Texas in 1886 and took possession of the road by the end of 1887, making it a sister line of the former MC&L. After acquiring the road, the L&N converted the line to its

David Newton Kennedy (1820–1904) was physically unable to fight during the Civil War, but he served in the Confederacy's treasury department. He was a staple of the Clarksville community and was involved in the MC&L and a later railroad, the Indiana, Alabama & Texas. *HathiTrust.*

standard gauge of four feet, nine inches. The road was later known as the Clarksville & Princeton Branch. The L&N abandoned the route following the May 13, 1933 run of a mixed train due to poor traffic over the line.

Meanwhile, a third railroad—the Tennessee Central—organized in the latter half of the nineteenth century. Its line was built from Harriman, Tennessee, to Hopkinsville, Kentucky, crossing the former MC&L line near the Cumberland River bridge. The unprofitable Tennessee Central ceased operations on August 31, 1968. At that time, a court-appointed trustee divided the railroad and sold its property to three competing railroads: the Illinois Central, the L&N and Southern Railway.

After the Tennessee Central shuttered, some of the railroad's locomotives were parked in Hopkinsville, Kentucky, news accounts suggest. The next day, the Illinois Central assumed the line's operations between Hopkinsville and Nashville. The line operated as part of the Illinois Central's—and, subsequently, the Illinois Central Gulf's—Evansville District. About a decade later, the railroad announced its intention to vacate its line through Middle Tennessee. By January 1981, a petition to close the line between Hopkinsville and Nashville had been filed with the Interstate Commerce Commission (ICC). The ICC approved the application in October 1983, according to a contemporary newspaper account.

As part of the closure, the L&N agreed to assume operations on a half mile of track in downtown Clarksville. By 1986, the railroad's entire Evansville District was either closed or sold. The U.S. Army later purchased a portion of the old Illinois Central Gulf line to service Fort Campbell, Kentucky. Other portions of the old Illinois Central Gulf line in Clarksville have since been turned into a walking trail. Former railroad bridges are visible throughout town, including one crossing Commerce Street near the police department's headquarters.

THE POST–MC&L LINE

One of the most significant events on the post–Memphis, Clarksville & Louisville line happened at about 8:00 p.m. on September 29, 1906. A northbound Louisville & Nashville passenger train—No. 102—steamed toward a swing bridge crossing the Cumberland River. Near the overpass, a glowing red light broke the darkness of the night, signaling for an approaching train to stop. The swing bridge was open, waiting for the steamboat *Buttoff* to pass through the opening on its way to Paducah, Kentucky.

Suddenly, engineer Frank Porter yanked on the Johnson bar, trying to reverse the locomotive before the train reached the open bridge. Sparks flew from the engine, and the train jolted but was unable to stop before the train's locomotive, its tender, a mail car and a baggage car plunged into the Cumberland River. The train's passenger coaches, however, remained on the trestle, with passengers panicking and trying to find a way out of the cars.

It was an "appalling catastrophe," proclaimed newspaper headlines. "It seems the cruel irony of fate that after the fearful disaster, immediately the draw was closed, and the steamer passed under the bridge without any trouble or hindrance, showing that there was no necessity for an open draw," stated an article that appeared in the *Clarksville Leaf-Chronicle* on October 1, 1906.

Porter and the train's express messenger—Will T. Wood—were the only two fatalities of the wreck. The train's fireman—John S. Moran—survived and "found himself clinging to an iron spike fastened to the masonry of a bridge pier," Dennis Mize wrote in his 1999 book, *L&N's Memphis Line*.[354]

"My first impression was that the train had stopped very suddenly and violently," said R.L. Morris, baggage master on the train. "I knew distinctively that this meant danger of some character....At the moment that I sensed danger, I ran to the back end of the car and started to jump, thinking that a terrible wreck was imminent. Then the car turned turtle and went down. It was all over so quickly that I have little recollection of subsequent events."[355]

In an interview with the *Clarksville Leaf-Chronicle*, Moran "had little to say, however, for he had no coherent recollection of anything from the moment the locomotive took the fatal leap until he found himself struggling for life in the deep, treacherous and swirling waters," the newspaper wrote.

"The last time I saw engineer Porter he was sitting on his seat box," Moran told the newspaper shortly after the wreck. "I was shoveling in coal, getting ready for the hill; doing this after we had blown for signal. No word was spoken either by Porter or myself. I was not looking for or paying any attention to the signals, and hence did not see them. We could not have been going more than four or five miles an hour when the engine went down."

The newspaper credited the train's air brakes with preventing a far worse catastrophe. If not for the system, the publication predicted, perhaps all of the train's cars would have plunged into the Cumberland River.

A similar tragedy happened four decades later on June 13, 1947, when an L&N locomotive and two freight cars carrying slag plunged from the open

A view of R.J. Corman's tracks heading toward the bridge over the Cumberland River in Clarksville around 2002. The railroad's freight depot was located in this area. *Railfanning.org*.

drawbridge into the river, sending steaming water hundreds of feet into the air. The wreck claimed the lives of engineer John Black and fireman M.E. "Red" Carter. Before the crash, the train, No. 117, which operated between Paris, Tennessee, and Guthrie, Kentucky, was switching cars in a nearby rail yard, then slowly rolled onto the bridge.

Ten years later, on June 29, 1957, an L&N wreck killed six people in Guthrie, Kentucky. Freight train No. 121 "crashed into the side of the Dixieland" at about 4:30 p.m. The L&N blamed the freight's fireman, George T. Smith, for the wreck, according to a July 20, 1957 story in the *Clarksville Leaf-Chronicle*.

L&N CHANGES

In 1957, the Louisville & Nashville subsumed the Nashville, Chattanooga & St. Louis, of which it had held a controlling interest since 1880. With the action, the L&N gained a direct line between Nashville and Memphis. However, that didn't mean the L&N would neglect the former MC&L line. On February 1, 1965, taller cars began operating over the line after the railroad enlarged the historic tunnel in Palmyra. This was done by lowering the tunnel's floor rather than raising its roof—a move that could save some trains a full twenty-four hours of travel time. As a part of the project, which began in November 1964, crews removed more than one thousand cubic yards of rock and dirt.[356]

In the 1960s, passenger travel decreased on the line, as it did across the country. The L&N ran the last Pan American train on November 15, 1965, ending daytime service on the line. The night train last ran on February 28, 1968, ending passenger traffic along the former MC&L route just a few years before Amtrak began its operations elsewhere in the country on May 1, 1971.

Despite the end of passenger travel, the L&N retained ownership of the railroad station and its butterfly shed on Tenth Street in downtown Clarksville. However, in 1978, the railroad petitioned to abandon the depot. The Tennessee Service Commission approved its request on October 3, 1979.

That same year, the Mid-Cumberland Council of Governments and the L&N struck an agreement "ending local opposition to the abandonment of the Tennessee River bridge on the railroad's Memphis Branch," according to a news release dated January 12, 1979. Local officials opposed the railroad's decision to abandon the bridge, fearing it might lead to total abandonment of the Memphis line. Since mid-1974, the L&N had used the former Nashville, Chattanooga & St. Louis Railway line between Nashville and Memphis, and in the January 12, 1979 release, officials indicated the L&N had used the Tennessee River bridge just nine times in the previous four years.

At the same time, according to the news release, the L&N assured local leaders that the railroad would continue to operate trains across the Cumberland River bridge in Clarksville. The railroad spent approximately $95,000 on the Clarksville bridge in the three years leading up to 1979.

A few years later, it looked as if the former MC&L had reached the end of the line. Freight traffic operating on the line had dried up, and by March 1986, L&N successor Seaboard Systems was tearing up rails in Houston County. Much like it did a century earlier, the MC&L's story paralleled that of the nation's railroads, and again, the route struggled to survive.

Just as the future of the historic route looked bleak, the next year, Seaboard successor CSX reached an agreement with R.J. Corman to sell sixty-two miles of track from South Union, Kentucky, to Zinc, Tennessee, thereby preserving a large portion of the former MC&L route.[357] The sale signaled the start of a new day for the line, and with this action, life returned to this historic route for a new generation.

THE MODERN ERA

The newest era for the Memphis, Clarksville & Louisville began on October 12, 1999, when R.J. Corman officials and county officials boarded the train at the Tenth Street depot and rode to Cumberland City, about twenty miles west of Clarksville. They were celebrating the inaugural run of a train to Cumberland City. Officials told the *Leaf-Chronicle* they expected the newly rebuilt line to help the economies of Montgomery, Stewart and Houston Counties.

"This is an opportunity for industry development they wouldn't have because the railroad was abandoned years ago," said R.J. Corman, the line's then-president, who flew in via helicopter from Nicholasville, Kentucky, to witness the event. "This is a chance for service beyond Clarksville. As we look to the future, this area will prosper."[358]

R.J. Corman, which built a new facility in Guthrie, Kentucky, where it interchanged with CSX, served at least two plants—a zinc plant on the

An R.J. Corman GP16 locomotive is parked outside the engine house in Guthrie, Kentucky, in August 2002. *Railfanning.org.*

Cumberland River and Standard Gypsum in Cumberland City. The future of Clarksville's railroads—and, specifically, the former MC&L route—hinges on freight traffic, although bringing commuter rail to the city (and possibly the old MC&L line) has been floated as an option as traffic increases in the region.

Starting in 2004, R.J. Corman worked with a zinc production company to develop an intermodal port on the Cumberland River in Clarksville. Initially estimated to cost approximately $7.5 million, the project's cost ballooned to $11 million, and in 2017, R.J. Corman announced it was withdrawing from the project.

In 2006, the first phase of commuter rail service in Middle Tennessee opened between Lebanon and Nashville. A line between Clarksville and Nashville, however, isn't likely to be opened anytime soon. Rail service to other Middle Tennessee cities, such as Murfreesboro, is considered a higher priority and is likely to be completed first.

In 2009, the State of Tennessee gave Montgomery County $945,926 to help refurbish the historic Cumberland River bridge. The project aimed to

A former R.J. Corman locomotive was on display in front of the historic L&N depot in downtown Clarksville in 2012. While rivers helped shape Clarksville's early history, thanks to The Monkees and their 1966 single, "Last Train to Clarksville," the city is forever linked with railroads. The song, however, most likely isn't about any specific Clarksville. *Railfanning.org*.

help improve the bridge's structural integrity and safety while also helping with economic development and urban renewal efforts.[359]

While discussion continues regarding the future of service along the line, it is interesting to note that of the three rail lines built through Clarksville, only the MC&L remains. The route is a survivor. While men, women and children no longer flock to the tracks in the hopes of witnessing the "wonder of the age," that doesn't render the line any less essential or negate the line's importance to communities since its incorporation more than 165 years ago.

The historic bridge over the Cumberland River remains a centerpiece of Clarksville. The former L&N Depot at the intersection of Tenth and Commerce Streets is also a landmark, even if many people have never heard of the MC&L and have no idea about the long tracks the railroad left in its wake.

11

POSTSCRIPT

T he story of the Memphis, Clarksville & Louisville is not compelling because the railroad was revolutionary. It was not the first to carve a tunnel or build a bridge over a river. It did not play an especially major role in the Civil War. If anything, it was overshadowed from its inception by larger lines, mainly the Louisville & Nashville, which ultimately purchased the line. When writing the complete history of nineteenth-century railroads, this particular company occupies a position of "me too"—not a trailblazing one.

The railroad touched so many members of the local community, but the names of many associated with the railroad are lost to history. Others, like local resident Rufus J. Goostree, earned brief mentions for their connection with the railroad.

Goostree moved to Montgomery County in 1859 and worked as a contractor on the railroad, completing "his work in a satisfactory manner," W.P. Titus noted in his 1887 history, *Picturesque Clarksville, Past and Present: A History of the City of the Hills*. During the Civil War, Goostree served in the Fourteenth Tennessee Infantry. He was wounded at Petersburg but continued his Confederate service. He surrendered with General Lee's army at Appomattox Court House in Virginia. Following the war, he returned to Middle Tennessee and engaged in farming and later served on the Tobacco Board of Trade.[360]

In many ways, the story of the MC&L is that of southern railroads in the mid-nineteenth century. It struggled to complete its route, was devastated

R.J. Corman freight cars are shown parked in Clarksville in April 2002. The Kentucky-based railroad still runs over a portion of the former MC&L and interchanges with CSX in Guthrie. *Railfanning.org*.

during the Civil War and struggled to pull itself from the ashes during Reconstruction. Before long, it faded into the pages of history. Just a small portion of its former route remains today.

As MC&L president G.A. Henry noted in January 1855: "We are willing to do the work and our hands ought not to be tied and our energies paralyzed by divided counsels at one end of the road or at the other. The work is a great one, and it will not only take a strong pull to accomplish it but a 'pull all together.'"

To borrow a phrase from the November 1, 1861 edition of the *Clarksville Chronicle*, the railroad was "the great highway of travel" connecting north and south. The line left its indelible mark on the city, region and state. If its legacy as a survivor holds true, the line will be a vital part of the landscape for years to come.

In an August 1959 thesis, Samuel J. Winters aptly summed up the railroad's brief history: "The Memphis, Clarksville, and Louisville Railroad seems to have been one of those unfortunate organizations that was established at the wrong place at the wrong time—in the path of the Civil War." The railroad, Winters added, "was not able to pull itself up by its boot straps—so to speak—after the war, and seemed to make little, if any, progress under the hands of the receiver."[361]

In May 1870, a committee investigating the railroad asked former receiver S.B. Brown why, if the L&N and the Memphis & Ohio were able to make money, the MC&L was not. Brown responded, in his official testimony: "The two ends of the line have very great advantages over the Memphis, Clarksville and Louisville road; the two former having a large local trade and liberal equipments, while the Memphis, Clarksville and Louisville road has but little local trade and very limited equipments."

From the inception of the MC&L, it seemed inevitable that the L&N would purchase or assume control of it. The MC&L sought financial assistance from the L&N as early as 1853, just a year after its incorporation.

What's so interesting about studying this railroad is the intense optimism surrounding so much of the coverage of it. While local newspaper reporters of the day might be forgiven for their perpetually optimistic view of the railroad and its progress, a modern journalist might marvel at the positive tone in so many articles concerning the railroad.

A February 1866 article discussing the Memphis & Ohio and entire Memphis-to-Louisville line in *DeBow's Review* perfectly illustrates the level of optimism: "The short time that has elapsed since the opening of this route, and the partial prostration of trade in consequence of the war, precludes the formation of a correct estimate of the immense business that will be transacted by this road when peace shall again be restored."

While near the end of the nineteenth century, county officials took time to look back and explain the railroad's financial legacy, no one, it seems, took a moment to ask what could have been. How would the railroad have fared if there was no Civil War, or if the war had progressed differently? Would the route have survived—or perhaps even thrived?

While it is impossible to say what might have happened, the end result likely would be unchanged. Maybe the railroad would have remained independent for longer, but at some point, one would have to surmise, the L&N would have purchased the line and subsumed it into the larger Memphis Branch, as it did.

To be sure, the route itself was an important one. Hence, it remained a single entity under the L&N and its successors for the better part of 125 years. The MC&L's shortfall was that it could not operate independently of its connecting lines.

The railroad started with such promise. It was to be a great connection to the outside world. In the annals of history, it is merely a footnote, and barely

The historic L&N depot, pictured here in 2012, stands in downtown Clarksville at the intersection of Commerce and Tenth Streets. *Railfanning.org.*

that. Historians do not study this railroad. It played no larger role in the development of the nation's network. It was hardly cutting-edge in anything it did. Yet, its footprint can still be seen today, including an engineering marvel of a bridge across the Cumberland River in downtown Clarksville.

The Memphis, Clarksville & Louisville was like so many other lines born of a fever to construct railroads in every direction. It was the first of three railroads built through Clarksville, and more than 150 years after its incorporation, this line is the only one that remains in the city. And it's all thanks to a few men whom history has all but forgotten.

NOTES

Chapter 1

1. "The First Trip over the Bridge!" *Clarksville (TN) Chronicle*, August 10, 1860.
2. "The Memphis Branch Railroad," *Louisville Daily Courier*, October 5, 1858.
3. Clark, *Beginning of the L&N*.
4. Klein, *History of the Louisville & Nashville Railroad*.
5. Clark, *Beginning of the L&N*.
6. Toplovich, "Cumberland River."
7. McLeod, "Thomas Walker."
8. Titus, *Picturesque Clarksville*.
9. Ibid.
10. DeFeo, "History: County Carved by Rivers, War."
11. Williams, "Montgomery County."
12. Todd DeFeo, "Clarksville's Poston Building Reminds of City's Former Cash Crop," *Travel Trolley*, May 3, 2010, http://thetraveltrolley. com/2010/05/clarksvilles-poston-building-reminds-of-citys-former-cash-crop/.
13. Winters, "History of the Memphis, Clarksville, and Louisville Railroad."
14. Titus, *Picturesque Clarksville*.
15. *Clarksville (TN) Weekly Chronicle*, May 28, 1881.
16. "The Ante-Bellum History of the M. C. & L. Railroad Company," *Clarksville (TN) Weekly Chronicle*, May 28, 1881.
17. "The Road to Hopkinsville," *Clarksville (TN) Chronicle*, April 14, 1846.

18. "The Raod [*sic*] to Hopkinsville," *Clarksville (TN) Chronicle*, April 21, 1846.

19. *Morning Courier and American Democrat* (Louisville, KY), May 15, 1846.

20. "Ante-Bellum History of the M. C. & L."

21. "Meeting," *Clarksville (TN) Jeffersonian*, May 14, 1851.

Chapter 2

22. Acts of the State of Tennessee, Passed at the First Session of the Twenty-Ninth General Assembly (accessed via Google Books)

23. Lindsay, "Memphis Branch of the Louisville & Nashville Railroad."

24. Addie Lou Brooks, "The Building of the Trunk Line Railroads in West Tennessee, 1852–1861," *Tennessee Historical Quarterly* 1, no. 2 (1942): 99–124, www.jstor.org/stable/42620738.

25. Clark, *Beginning of the L&N.*

26. Ibid.

27. *Louisville Daily Courier*, April 12, 1852.

28. Ibid.

29. Ibid.

30. *Louisville Daily Courier*, April 27, 1852.

31. *Daily Picayune* (New Orleans, LA), June 7, 1853.

32. "Ante-Bellum History of the M. C. & L."

33. *Daily Picayune* (New Orleans, LA), June 7, 1853.

34. "Ante-Bellum History of the M. C. & L."

35. Klein, *History of the Louisville & Nashville Railroad.*

36. "Vote on Railroad Tax," *Louisville Daily Courier*, October 26, 1853.

37. Ibid.

38. Brooks, "Building of the Trunk Line Railroads."

39. "Railroad Directors," *Clarksville (TN) Jeffersonian*, May 31, 1854.

40. *Republican Banner* (Nashville, TN), December 22, 1854.

41. *Clarksville (TN) Jeffersonian*, January 24, 1855.

42. *Republican Banner* (Nashville, TN), December 22, 1854.

43. *Clarksville (TN) Jeffersonian*, January 24, 1855.

44. "Ante-Bellum History of the M. C. & L."

45. "Munford, William B.," Montgomery County Biographical Directory, www.tngenweb.org/montgomery/biodir/wmunfordbio.html, accessed July 31, 2018.

46. "Ante-Bellum History of the M. C. & L."

47. "The Rail Road put to Contract," *Clarksville (TN) Jeffersonian*, April 30, 1856.

48. Ibid.

49. "The Upper and Lower Route," *Clarksville (TN) Jeffersonian*, April 30, 1856.

50. *Clarksville (TN) Jeffersonian*, May 14, 1856.

51. "The Railroad Meeting," *Clarksville (TN) Jeffersonian*, May 21, 1856.

52. "Ante-Bellum History of the M. C. & L."

53. Ibid.

54. *Clarksville (TN) Jeffersonian*, June 11, 1856.

55. "To Rail Road Contractors," *Clarksville (TN) Jeffersonian*, June 18, 1856.

56. "The Work on the Railroad Commenced," *Clarksville (TN) Jeffersonian*, June 25, 1856.

57. *Louisville Daily Courier*, July 7, 1856.

58. "Work on the Railroad Commenced."

59. "Loyal to the Core," *Daily Tobacco Leaf–Chronicle* (Clarksville, TN), September 17, 1897.

60. "The Rail Road," *Clarksville (TN) Jeffersonian*, January 14, 1857.

61. "The Rail Road," *Clarksville (TN) Jeffersonian*, February 18, 1857.

62. Brooks, "Beginning of Railroads in West Tennessee."

63. Ibid.

64. "Our Railroad in Jeopardy," *Clarksville (TN) Jeffersonian*, October 14, 1857.

65. R.G. Payne.

66. "Ante-Bellum History of the M. C. & L."

67. *Clarksville (TN) Chronicle*, February 12, 1858.

68. Ibid.

69. "The Memphis Branch Railroad," *Louisville Daily Courier*, October 5, 1858.

70. "Consolidation," *Clarksville (TN) Jeffersonian*, April 28, 1858.

71. *Clarksville (TN) Chronicle*, May 7, 1858.

72. "Railroad," *Clarksville (TN) Chronicle*, July 2, 1858.

73. Mize, *L&N's Memphis Line*.

74. "Railroad."

75. "The Memphis Branch Railroad," *Clarksville (TN) Chronicle*, October 22, 1858.

76. "Clarksville Railroad," *Republican Banner* (Nashville, TN), September 25, 1858.

77. "Memphis, Clarksville and Louisville Railroad," *Republican Banner* (Nashville, TN), December 22, 1858.
78. "Louisville All Right," *Clarksville (TN) Jeffersonian*, November 10, 1858.
79. Ibid.
80. *Clarksville (TN) Chronicle*, March 25, 1859.
81. Ibid.
82. "Palmyra Tunnel," *Clarksville (TN) Jeffersonian*, April 13, 1859.
83. *Clarksville (TN) Chronicle*, May 20, 1859.
84. Ibid.
85. Ibid.
86. *Clarksville (TN) Jeffersonian*, June 29, 1859.
87. Ibid.
88. *Clarksville (TN) Chronicle*, May 6, 1859.
89. Mize, *L&N's Memphis Line*.
90. *Clarksville (TN) Chronicle*, May 20, 1859.
91. Ibid.

Chapter 3

92. *Clarksville (TN) Chronicle*, June 3, 1859.
93. *Clarksville (TN) Chronicle*, September 30, 1859.
94. *Clarksville (TN) Chronicle*, November 4, 1859.
95. *Clarksville (TN) Jeffersonian*, December 1859.
96. *Clarksville (TN) Jeffersonian*, January 25, 1860.
97. *Clarksville (TN) Chronicle*, July 30, 1858.
98. *Clarksville (TN) Chronicle*, October 22, 1858.
99. Ibid.
100. Irene Griffey, "Cumberland Railroad Bridge, 1860–2008," *The Leaf-Chronicle Cumberland Lore*, February 8, 2008.
101. Poor, *History of the Railroads and Canals of the United States of America*.
102. *Clarksville (TN) Chronicle*, December 3, 1858.
103. *Clarksville (TN) Chronicle*, August 19, 1859.
104. *Clarksville (TN) Chronicle*, December 16, 1859.
105. Ibid.
106. "River and Steamboat Matters," *Clarksville (TN) Chronicle*, December 23, 1859.
107. "Steamboat Accident," *Nashville Patriot*, December 22, 1859.

108. "River and Steamboat News," *Nashville Union and American*, December 22, 1859.

109. *Nashville Union and American.*, October 28, 1860.

110. "Railroad Items," *Clarksville (TN) Jeffersonian*, February 1, 1860.

111. "Railroad from Clarksville to Nashville," *Clarksville (TN) Jeffersonian*, March 14, 1860.

112. *Clarksville (TN) Jeffersonian*, April 18, 1860.

113. "Memphis, Clarksville and Louisville Railroad," *Republican Banner* (Nashville, TN), March 10, 1860.

114. Brooks, "Building of the Trunk Line Railroads."

115. *Clarksville (TN) Chronicle*, May 4, 1860.

116. *Clarksville (TN) Jeffersonian*, May 30, 1860.

117. "A Frightful Accident," *Clarksville (TN) Jeffersonian*, May 16, 1860.

118. "The Accident Repeated," *Clarksville (TN) Jeffersonian*, May 16, 1860.

119. "Narrow Escape," *Clarksville (TN) Jeffersonian*, July 11, 1860.

120. *Clarksville (TN) Chronicle*, July 27, 1860.

121. Ibid.

122. *Clarksville (TN) Chronicle*, June 8, 1860.

123. Ibid.

124. "Memphis, Clarksville & Louisville Railroad Locomotives," Confederate Railroad Maps, accessed June 8, 2018, www.csa-railroads. com/Memphis,_Clarksville_and_Louisville_Locomotives.htm.

125. "The Cumberland River Bridge," *Clarksville (TN) Jeffersonian*, July 25, 1860.

126. "The First Trip over the Bridge!" *Clarksville (TN) Chronicle*, August 10, 1860. Paragraphs added by author.

127. "The Crossing of the Cumberland," *Clarksville (TN) Jeffersonian*, August 8, 1860.

128. "The Railroad Banquet," *Clarksville (TN) Chronicle*, September 21, 1860.

129. Ibid.

130. Ibid.

131. *Clarksville (TN) Chronicle*, October 19, 1860.

132. *Clarksville (TN) Chronicle*, October 26, 1860.

133. *American Railroad Journal*, October 27, 1860.

134. *Clarksville (TN) Jeffersonian*, October 31, 1860.

135. *Clarksville (TN) Chronicle*, November 9, 1860.

136. "Memphis, Louisville and Clarksville," *Louisville Daily Courier*, November 16, 1860.

137. *Clarksville (TN) Chronicle*, February 10, 1860.

138. *Clarksville (TN) Chronicle*, November 23, 1860.

139. "Through to Memphis," *Clarksville (TN) Jeffersonian*, January 16, 1861.

140. *Clarksville (TN) Chronicle*, January 25, 1861.

141. "Louisville and Memphis Railroad," *Nashville Patriot*, October 23, 1860.

142. *Clarksville (TN) Chronicle*, January 25, 1861.

143. "Accident," *Clarksville (TN) Jeffersonian*, February 20, 1861.

144. "A Trip to the Tennessee River," *Clarksville (TN) Jeffersonian*, February 20, 1861.

145. Ibid.

146. "Two Tracts of Land," *Clarksville (TN) Jeffersonian*, January 30, 1861.

147. *Clarksville (TN) Chronicle*, February 15, 1861.

148. *Clarksville (TN) Jeffersonian*, February 20, 1861.

149. "Appointment," *Clarksville (TN) Jeffersonian*, March 27, 1861.

150. *Clarksville (TN) Jeffersonian*, April 3, 1861.

151. *Clarksville (TN) Jeffersonian*, March 13, 1861.

152. "The Great Southern Mail Route," *Clarksville (TN) Jeffersonian*, March 6, 1861.

153. Ibid.

154. *Clarksville (TN) Chronicle*, April 5, 1861.

155. *Clarksville (TN) Jeffersonian*, January 30, 1861.

156. *Clarksville (TN) Jeffersonian*, May 29, 1861.

157. "A Smash Up," *Clarksville (TN) Jeffersonian*, May 8, 1861.

158. *Clarksville (TN) Jeffersonian*, May 22, 1861.

159. *Clarksville (TN) Chronicle* , March 15, 1861.

160. "Finished," *Clarksville (TN) Chronicle* , November 8, 1861.

161. Mize, *L&N's Memphis Line*.

162. Ibid.

163. Titus, *Picturesque Clarksville*.

Chapter 4

164. "Louisville and Memphis Railroad," *Louisville Daily Courier*, April 12, 1861.

165. Bell, "I've Been Working On the Railroad."

166. "Contraband of War," *Clarksville (TN) Jeffersonian*, May 15, 1861.

167. *Clarksville (TN) Chronicle*, June 7, 1861.

168. *Clarksville (TN) Chronicle*, July 12, 1861.

169. "Heavy Travel," *Clarksville (TN) Chronicle*, May 3, 1861.

170. *Clarksville (TN) Chronicle,* July 12, 1861.

171. Ash, "A Community at War."

172. Ibid.

173. "Notice to Military Companies," *Clarksville (TN) Jeffersonian,* July 9, 1861.

174. *Clarksville (TN) Chronicle.* July 12, 1861.

175. "Rail Road," *Clarksville (TN) Chronicle,* July 26, 1861.

176. *Clarksville (TN) Chronicle,* October 18, 1861. This table is not produced verbatim.

177. "New Regulations," *Clarksville (TN) Chronicle,* September 13, 1861.

178. "Villainy," *Clarksville (TN) Jeffersonian,* October 22, 1861.

179. *Clarksville (TN) Jeffersonian,* October 22, 1861.

180. "All Right," *Clarksville (TN) Chronicle,* October 25, 1861.

181. *Nashville Union and American,* October 22, 1861.

182. "The Bridge," *Clarksville (TN) Chronicle,* November 1, 1861.

183. "Railroad Accident," *Clarksville (TN) Jeffersonian,* December 20, 1861.

184. "Accidents," *Clarksville (TN) Jeffersonian,* January 2, 1862.

185. U.S. War Department, *The War of the Rebellion.*

186. Ibid.

187. "Railroad Matters," *Clarksville (TN) Chronicle,* January 10, 1862.

188. "Defence of Cumberland," *Republican Banner* (Nashville, TN), November 2, 1861.

189. U.S. Congressional Serial Set, Volume 1706, accessed via Google Books.

190. U.S. War Department, *The War of the Rebellion.*

191. Williams, "Montgomery County."

192. "Gen. Halleck's Department," *New York Times,* February 19, 1862.

193. Bell, "I've Been Working On the Railroad."

194. Report of the Secretary of the Navy in Relation to Armored Vessels (accessed via Google Books).

195. "The Campaign in Tennessee," *New York Times,* February 23, 1862.

196. U.S. Naval War Records Office, "Official Records of the Union and Confederate Navies in the War of the Rebellion," U.S. Government Printing Office, Washington, D.C., 1908.

197. Johnson, *The Papers of Andrew Johnson.*

198. Ibid.

199. *Travelers Guide to the Louisville & Nashville Railroad* (Louisville, KY: Lucas & Co., 1867).

200. Herr, *Louisville & Nashville Railroad;* Mize, *L&N's Memphis Line.*

201. *Clarksville (TN) Gazette*, February 10, 1864.
202. Ibid.
203. "The M., C. & L. R. R," *Clarksville (TN) Chronicle*, July 28, 1865.
204. "An Interesting Letter from Kentucky," *Nashville Daily Union*, August 15, 1865.
205. *Clarksville (TN) Weekly Chronicle*, September 29, 1865.
206. *Clarksville (TN) Chronicle*, November 24, 1865.
207. Louisville and Nashville Railroad Company, *Annual Report of the Board of Directors of the Louisville & Nashville Railroad Company to the Stockholders* (Louisville, KY, 1888).

Chapter 5

208. *Clarksville (TN) Leaf-Chronicle*, July 20, 1870.
209. State of Tennessee, *State of Tennessee and the United States: Extracts from records, journals and documents, for use in the matters of controversy referred to in House joint resolution no. 25, acts of Tennessee* (Nashville, TN: Brandon Printing Company).
210. U.S. Military Railroad Department, *United States Military Railroads: Report of Bvt. Brig. Gen. D.C. McCallum, Director And General Manager, From 1861 to 1866*, Washington, D.C., 1866.
211. *Clarksville (TN) Weekly Chronicle*, November 10, 1865.
212. *Clarksville (TN) Chronicle*, November 10, 1865.
213. *Clarksville (TN) Weekly Chronicle*, December 1, 1865.
214. *Clarksville (TN) Chronicle*, December 1, 1865.
215. Ibid.
216. "Our Railroad," *Clarksville (TN) Weekly Chronicle*, February 9, 1866.
217. "River News," *Clarksville (TN) Weekly Chronicle*, February 9, 1866.
218. "Our Railroad," *Clarksville (TN) Weekly Chronicle*, February 9, 1866.
219. Testimony Taken Before the Judiciary Committee of the House of Representatives in the Investigation of the Charges Against Andrew Johnson: Second Session Thirty-Ninth Congress, and First Session Fortieth Congress, 1867 (accessed via Google Books).
220. Ibid.
221. *Clarksville (TN) Weekly Chronicle*, March 23, 1866.
222. Testimony Taken Before the Judiciary Committee of the House of Representatives in the Investigation of the Charges Against Andrew Johnson.

223. House Documents, Volume 4, Volume 234.

224. "The Railroad Bridge Accident," *Clarksville (TN) Weekly Chronicle*, May 25, 1866.

225. "Letter From George T. Lewis to Gov. Brownlow," *Clarksville (TN) Weekly Chronicle*, May 25, 1866.

226. "The Memphis, Clarksville and Louisville Railroad," *Louisville Daily Courier*, May 23, 1866.

227. "Election," *Clarksville (TN) Weekly Chronicle*, May 18, 1866.

228. *Clarksville (TN) Leaf-Chronicle*, July 20, 1870.

229. "Letter From George T. Lewis to Gov. Brownlow," *Clarksville (TN) Weekly Chronicle*, May 25, 1866.

230. "Report of Geo. T. Lewis," *Clarksville (TN) Chronicle*, September 21, 1866.

231. Ibid.

232. Ibid.

233. *Annual Report of the Louisville & Nashville R.R. Co., 1866–67.*

234. "Railroad Jollification," *Clarksville (TN) Chronicle*, July 27, 1866.

235. "Memphis, Clarksville and Louisville Railroad," *Clarksville (TN) Weekly Chronicle*, August 10, 1866.

236. "Report of Geo. T. Lewis," *Clarksville (TN) Chronicle*, September 21, 1866.

237. Ibid. This table is not a verbatim transcription of the report.

238. The Reports of the Committees of the House of Representatives Made During the Second Session Thirty-Ninth Congress (accessed via Google Books).

239. "Important Railroad Meeting," *Public Ledger* (Memphis, TN), August 3, 1866.

240. "Personal," *Clarksville (TN) Weekly Chronicle*, August 17, 1866.

241. "Railroad Hotel," *Clarksville (TN) Weekly Chronicle*, November 16, 1866.

242. "Thanks," *Clarksville (TN) Weekly Chronicle*, November 30, 1866.

243. "M. C. & L. Railroad," *Clarksville (TN) Weekly Chronicle*, December 21, 1866.

244. Louisville & Nashville Railroad, *Annual Report of the Louisville & Nashville R.R. Co.* (Louisville, KY: John P. Morton & Co., 1867).

245. *Clarksville (TN) Chronicle*, April 19, 1867.

246. *Travelers Guide to the Louisville & Nashville Railroad.*

247. Louisville & Nashville Railroad, *Annual Report of the Louisville & Nashville R.R. Co.* (Louisville, KY: John P. Morton & Co., 1867).

248. "Dreadful Railroad Accident," *Natchez (MS) Daily Courier*, December 13, 1866.

249. "Another Fatal Railroad Accident," *Nashville Union and Dispatch*, December 9, 1866.

250. *Annual Report of the Louisville & Nashville R.R. Co., 1866–67*.

251. *Clarksville (TN) Leaf-Chronicle*, July 20, 1870.

252. *Clarksville (TN) Weekly Chronicle*, March 15, 1867.

253. Ibid.

254. *W.H. Bristol & Thomas Skidmore v. Memphis, Clarksville, & Louisville Railroad Co.*

255. Ibid.

256. Winters, "History of the Memphis, Clarksville, and Louisville Railroad."

257. *Clarksville (TN) Weekly Chronicle*, July 5, 1867.

258. "The Legislature," *Nashville Union and Dispatch*, February 4, 1868.

259. *Clarksville (TN) Leaf-Chronicle*, July 20, 1870.

260. Letter from G.A. Henry, et al., to W.G. Brownlow, January 25,1868.

261. "Strike Among Railroad Employes," *Detroit Free Press*, February 2, 1868.

262. *Clarksville (TN) Chronicle*, February 7, 1868.

263. Herr, *Louisville & Nashville Railroad*.

Chapter 6

264. Ibid.

265. "Message From the Governor," *Clarksville (TN) Chronicle*, February 21, 1868.

266. *Clarksville (TN) Chronicle*, February 21, 1868.

267. "The Memphis, Clarksville and Louisville Railroad—Destitution of the Late Employees," *Nashville Union and Dispatch*, February 9, 1868. Paragraphs added by the author.

268. Klein, *History of the Louisville & Nashville Railroad*.

269. "M. C. & L. R. R," *Clarksville (TN) Chronicle*, February 28, 1868.

270. Henry V. Poor, *Manual of the Railroads of the United States 1869–70* (New York: H.V. & H.W. Poor).

271. Ibid.

272. "Important Railroad Suit," *Nashville Union and American*, November 15, 1870.

273. "Case of the Memphis, Clarksville and Louisville," *Republican Banner* (Nashville, TN), August 21, 1868.

274. *Annual Report of the Louisville & Nashville Railroad Company, 1868–69*.

Chapter 7

275. "Late Railroad Disaster," *Public Ledger* (Memphis, TN), July 29, 1869.

276. "The Railroad Disaster," *Clarksville (TN) Chronicle*, July 31, 1869.

277. "Fearful Railroad Disaster," *Federal Union* (Milledgeville, GA), August 10, 1869.

278. "More of the R. R. Disaster," *Louisville Evening Express*, July 29, 1869.

279. Ibid.

280. Ibid.

281. "The Railroad Disaster," *Clarksville (TN) Chronicle*, July 31, 1869.

282. "The Late Railroad Disaster in Tennessee," *The Sun* (Baltimore, MD), August 2, 1869.

283. "From Budd's Creek," *Public Ledger* (Memphis, TN), August 2, 1869.

284. "Railroad Disaster," *Lafayette (LA) Advertiser*, August 21, 1869; "Late Railroad Disaster," *Public Ledger* (Memphis, TN), July 29, 1869.

285. "More of the R. R. Disaster."

286. "More of the R. R. Disaster."

287. Ibid.

288. "The Disaster on the Memphis and Louisville Railroad," *Daily Picayune* (New Orleans, LA), August 3, 1869.

289. "Late Railroad Disaster in Tennessee."

290. "The Railroad Disaster," *Public Ledger* (Memphis, TN), July 30, 1869.

291. *Clarksville (TN) Chronicle*, October 25, 1861.

292. "Paying on Baggage Lost at Rudd's Creek," *Courier-Journal* (Louisville, KY), August 1–2, 1869.

293. *Fort Wayne (IN) Daily Gazette*, July 29, 1869.

294. "Frightful Disaster" *Republican Banner* (Nashville, TN), July 29, 1869.

295. *History of the Illinois Central Railroad Company and Representative Employes* (Chicago: Railroad Historical Company, 1900).

296. Woodruff-Fontaine House Museum history, accessed October 30, 2018, www.woodruff-fontaine.org/history.

297. *Public Ledger* (Memphis, TN), August 14, 1869.

298. *Portrait and Biographical Album of Hillsdale County, Mich.* (Chicago: Chapman Brothers, 1888).

299. "The Late Railroad Disaster," *Nashville Union and American*, August 11, 1869.

300. "From Budd's Creek."

301. "Our Late Railroad Disaster," *Clarksville (TN) Tobacco Leaf*, September 6, 1869.

302. "Bowling Green," *Courier-Journal* (Louisville, KY), August 1–2, 1869.

303. *Republican Banner* (Nashville, TN), November 5, 1869.

304. *Clarksville (TN) Tobacco Leaf*, July, 20, 1870.

305. *Annual Report of the Louisville & Nashville Railroad Company, 1868–69.*

306. Ibid.

307. "The Last Railroad Accident," *Galveston (TX) Daily News*, August 3, 1869.

308. "Arrest of a Young Thief," *Louisville Evening Express*, August 2, 1869.

309. "A Train Boy in Trouble," *Courier-Journal* (Louisville, KY), August 3, 1869.

310. "Train-boy Nolan Discharged," *Courier-Journal* (Louisville, KY), August 5, 1869.

311. "Chamber of Commerce," *Daily Picayune* (New Orleans, LA), September 8, 1869.

312. *Clarksville (TN) Chronicle*, July 31, 1869.

313. *Clarksville (TN) Chronicle*, August 7, 1869.

314. "Railroad Accidents," *Republican Banner* (Nashville, TN), September 1, 1869.

315. "Railroad Accident," *Nashville Union and American*, September 1, 1869.

316. "J. J. Buck vs. L. & N. R. R," *Clarksville (TN) Weekly Chronicle*, January 24, 1874.

Chapter 8

317. "Railroad News," *Clarksville (TN) Tobacco Leaf*, December 1, 1869.

318. *Clarksville (TN) Tobacco Leaf*, January 5, 1870.

319. Poor, *Manual of the Railroads of the United States 1871–72.*

320. *Annual Report of the Louisville & Nashville R.R. Co., 1869–70.*

321. Henry V. Poor, *Manual of the Railroads of the United States 1870–71* (New York: H.V. & H.W. Poor).

322. *Annual Report of the Louisville & Nashville R.R. Co., 1869–70.*

323. "Terrible Explosion," *Clarksville (TN) Chronicle*, February 12, 1870; "Serious Railroad Accident—Three Men Killed," *Republican Banner* (Nashville, TN), February 11, 1870.

324. "Terrible Explosion."

325. Ibid.

326. *Clarksville (TN) Tobacco Leaf*, July 20, 1870.

327. Tennessee General Assembly, *Memphis, Clarksville & Louisville R. R.: Report of the Joint Select Committee to Investigate the Affairs of the Railroads in Tennessee* (Nashville, TN: Jones, Purvis &, 1870).

328. "Increased Earnings of the M. C. and L. Road," *Clarksville (TN) Tobacco Leaf*, December 14, 1870.

329. *New Orleans Republican*, October 30, 1870.

330. *Clarksville (TN) Chronicle*, January 14, 1871.

331. "M. C. & L. Railroad," *Clarksville (TN) Chronicle*, May 27, 1871.

332. "The Railroad Suit," *Republican Banner* (Nashville, TN), April 7, 1871.

333. "Settled at Last," *Republican Banner* (Nashville, TN), July 9, 1871.

334. State of Tennessee, *State of Tennessee and the United States: Extracts from records, journals and documents, for use in the matters of controversy referred to in House joint resolution no. 25, acts of Tennessee* (Nashville, TN: Brandon Printing Company).

335. "Purchase of the State's Interest in the Memphis, Charleston and Louisville Railroad," *Republican Banner* (Nashville, TN), October 3, 1871.

336. Prince, *Louisville & Nashville Steam Locomotives*.

337. *Memphis (TN) Daily Appeal*, October 7, 1872.

Chapter 9

338. "Resolution of Thanks," *Clarksville (TN) Weekly Chronicle*, June 4, 1881.

339. "Grand Re-Union of the Ante-Bellum Officers and Contractors of the M. C. & L. R. R.," *Clarksville (TN) Weekly Chronicle*, May 7, 1881.

340. "Reunion of the Ante-Bellum Officers of the M., C. & L. R. R," *Clarksville (TN) Semi-Weekly Tobacco Leaf*, May 31, 1881.

341. "The Re-Union of the M. C. & L. Railroaders," *Clarksville (TN) Weekly Chronicle*, May 28, 1881.

342. "Ante-Bellum History of the M. C. & L."

343. "That Report," *Semi-Weekly Tobacco Leaf–Chronicle* (Clarksville, TN), April 11, 1890.

344. "Montgomery County's Victory," *Clarksville (TN) Tobacco Leaf*, March 21, 1878.

345. *Judith Simms, Burrell Williamson & wife v. Memphis, Clarksville, & Louisville Railroad Co.*

346. "That Report," *Semi-Weekly Tobacco Leaf–Chronicle* (Clarksville, TN), April 11, 1890.

347. "The Answer," *Semi-Weekly Tobacco Leaf–Chronicle* (Clarksville, TN), May 21, 1895. Paragraphs added by the author.

348. "Governor's Message," *Republican Banner* (Nashville, TN), March 13, 1872.

349. E.G. Campbell, "Indebted Railroads—A Problem of Reconstruction," *Journal of Southern History* 6, no. 2 (1940): 167–188, www.jstor.org/stable/2191204.

350. "Governor's Message," *Republican Banner* (Nashville, TN), March 13, 1872.

Chapter 10

351. "Passenger Depot Catches Fire," *Daily Tobacco Leaf–Chronicle* (Clarksville, TN), August 10, 1901.

352. "Railroad News," *Daily Tobacco Leaf–Chronicle* (Clarksville, TN), April 14, 1891.

353. "Our Contemplated Railroad," *Clarksville (TN) Weekly Chronicle*, February 25, 1882.

354. Mize, *L&N's Memphis Line.*

355. "An Appalling Catastrophe," *Clarksville (TN) Leaf-Chronicle*, October 1, 1906.

356. "Taller Freight Cars May Now Negotiate Tunnel," *Clarksville (TN) Leaf-Chronicle*, January 28, 1965.

357. "Corman Railroad on CSX Line," *Leaf-Chronicle* (Clarksville, TN), September 6, 1987.

358. "Take the Short-Line Train from Clarksville," *Leaf-Chronicle* (Clarksville, TN), October 13, 1999.

359. DeFeo, "Historic Tenn. Swing Bridge."

Postscript

360. Titus, *Picturesque Clarksville.*

361. Winters, "History of the Memphis, Clarksville, and Louisville Railroad."

Bibliography

American Railroad Journal. *American Railroad Journal, Volume 45*. New York: John H. Schultz, 1872.

Ash, Stephen V. "A Community at War: Montgomery County, 1861–65." *Tennessee Historical Quarterly* 36, no. 1 (1977): 30–43. http://www.jstor.org/stable/42623768.

Beach, Ursula Smith. *Along the Warioto*. Clarksville: Clarksville Kiwanis Club and the Tennessee Historical Commission, 1964.

Bell, Ira L. "I've Been Working On the Railroad" (speech given in Houston County, TN, in September 1994). http://www.rootsweb.com/~tnhousto/rail.htm.

Bright, David L. "Memphis, Clarksville & Louisville Locomotives." Confederate Railroads. Accessed June 8, 2018. http://www.csa-railroads.com/Memphis,_Clarksville_and_Louisville_Locomotives.htm.

Brooks, Addie Lou. "The Beginning of Railroads in West Tennessee, 1830–1861." Diss., Vanderbilt University, 1932.

Clark, Thomas Dionysius. *The Beginning of the L&N: The Development of the Louisville and Nashville Railroad and Its Memphis Branches from 1836 to 1860.* Louisville, KY: Standard Printing, 1933.

DeFeo, Todd. "An 'Appalling Catastrophe.'" Railfanning.org (blog). February 1, 2004.

———. "Church in Hunt for Historic Status." *The Tennessean*, September 23, 2002.

———. "Clarksville, Tenn., Railroad Strikes after Money Tightens." Railfanning.org (blog). January 15, 2003.

———. "Historic Tenn. Swing Bridge See Rehabilitation Funding." Railfanning.org (blog). September 7, 2009.

———. "History: County Carved by Rivers, War, Army and University." *Fact Book*, August 25, 2002: 12–16.

———. "Railroad Strike 135 Years Ago Left Long Tracks." *Clarksville (TN) Leaf-Chronicle*, February 23, 2003.

Herr, Kincaid. *The Louisville & Nashville Railroad: 1850–1963*. Louisville: University Press of Kentucky, 1964.

Johnson, Andrew. *The Papers of Andrew Johnson*. Vol. 5, 1861–1862. Knoxville: University of Tennessee Press, 1979.

Klein, Maury. *History of the Louisville & Nashville Railroad*. New York: Macmillan, 1972.

Lindsay, G.W. *Annual Report of the Louisville & Nashville Railroad Company, 1870–71*. Louisville, KY: John P. Morton & Co., 1871.

———. "The Memphis Branch of the Louisville & Nashville Railroad (1850–1871)." *Railway and Locomotive Historical Society Bulletin*, no. 81 (1950): 55–57.

Louisville & Nashville Railroad. *Annual Report of the Louisville & Nashville R.R. Co.* Louisville, KY: John P. Morton & Co., 1867.

———. *Annual Report of the President and Directors of of the Louisville & Nashville Railroad Company*. Louisville, KY: John P. Morton & Co., 1865.

———. *Travelers Guide to the Louisville & Nashville Railroad*. Louisville, KY: Lucas & Co., 1867.

McLeod, Alexander. "Thomas Walker." Tennessee Historical Society. October 8, 2017. Last modified March 1, 2018. http://www.tennesseeencyclopedia.net/entries/thomas-walker/.

Mead, H.E. *Kentucky and Tennessee. A Complete Guide to Their Railroads, Stations and Distances, Connections North and South; Their Rivers, Landings*. Louisville, KY: Self-published, 1867.

Mize, Dennis R. *L&N's Memphis Line: Bowling Green, Kentucky, to Memphis, Tennessee*. Port Charlotte, FL: MFS Line Publishing, 1999.

Poor, Henry Varnum. *History of the Railroads and Canals of the United States of America*. New York: John H. Schultz & Co., 1860.

———. *Manual of the Railroads of the United States 1871–72*. New York: H.V. & H.W. Poor, 1872.

———. *Poor's Manual of Railroads*. New York: H.V. & H.W. Poor, 1868.

Prince, Richard. *Louisville & Nashville Steam Locomotives.* Bloomington: Indiana University Press, 1968.

State of Tennessee. *Acts of the State of Tennessee Passed at the First Session of the Thirtieth General Assembly for the Years 1853–4.* Nashville: M'Kennie & Brown, 1854.

———. *Extracts from Records, Journals and Documents, for Use in the Matters of Controversy Referred to in House Joint Resolution No. 25, Acts of Tennessee, Page 498, Compiled September 24, 1895.* Nashville: Brandon Printing Company, 1895.

———. *State of Tennessee and the United States: Extracts from Records, Journals and Documents, for Use In the Matters of Controversy Referred to in House Joint Resolution No. 25, Acts of Tennessee.* Nashville: Brandon Printing Company, 1895.

Sulzer, Elmer G. *Ghost Railroads of Kentucky.* Bloomington: Indiana University Press, 1998.

———. *Ghost Railroads of Tennessee.* Bloomington: Indiana University Press, 1998.

Titus, W.P. *Picturesque Clarksville, Past and Present: A History of the City of the Hills.* 1887.

Toplovich, Ann. "Cumberland River." Tennessee Historical Society. October 8, 2017. Last modified March 1, 2018. http://www.tennesseeencyclopedia. net/entries/cumberland-river/.

U.S. Congress. *Testimony Taken Before the Judiciary Committee of the House of Representatives in the Investigation of the Charges Against Andrew Johnson.* Washington, D.C.: Government Printing Office, 1867.

U.S. Military Railroad Department. *United States Military Railroads: Report of Bvt. Brig. Gen. D.C. McCallum, Director and General Manager, from 1861 to 1866.* Washington, D.C.: U.S. Congress, 1866.

U.S. War Department. *The War of the Rebellion: A Compilation of the Official Records of the Union and Confederate Armies.* Washington, D.C.: Government Printing Office, 1900.

Williams, Eleanor. "Montgomery County." Tennessee Historical Society. October 8, 2017. Last modified March 1, 2018. http://www. tennesseeencyclopedia.net/entries/montgomery-county.

Winters, Samuel J. "A History of the Memphis, Clarksville, and Louisville Railroad in Montgomery County, Tennessee." Diss., Austin Peay State College, 1959.

Wurtele, Lolla. "The Origins of the Louisville and Nashville Railroad." Diss., University of Louisville, 1939.

Index

T

W

About the Author

T odd DeFeo has studied railroads since growing up alongside the Northeast Corridor in New Jersey. He is editor of Railfanning. org, a website dedicated to the railroad industry and its history, and founder of The DeFeo Groupe, an Atlanta-area content creation firm. A graduate of Denison University, located in Granville, Ohio, DeFeo earned a degree in history. As a newspaper reporter, he regularly wrote articles chronicling the history of the towns and communities he covered. One of his first such articles highlighted the Memphis, Clarksville & Louisville Railroad. In his spare time, he dabbles in folk music, writing songs about trains and other topics.